Consulting

The Discipline of Consulting

Everyday Practices
of
Extraordinary
Consultants

A Field Guide for Consultants

By
Christine Lambden
and
Casey Conner

Publisher: Red Line Publishing Group
                10601 FM 2222, Suite R-111
                Austin, Texas 78730

Dedications

To my dear wife, Kim,
whose support is my breath
whose faith in me is my heartbeat,
and whose patience with me is my freedom.
Kim, you're just....awesome.
Thank you, from the bottom of my heart.
Casey Conner

To my mother and sister,
who always have faith in me,
even when I'm not so sure.
Christine Lambden

A Note of Thanks

The lessons in this book were learned over twenty years in the consulting industry under the mentorship of many extraordinary consultants and managers. The book itself is the result of more than two years of conversation between the authors via instant message, telephone and face-to-face, often over adult beverages after a long day of practicing the discipline of consulting.

Even with all that experience, writing and editing this work required the combined efforts of many people. We especially wish to thank the following:

Kathleen Edwards, who contributed not only her attention and wisdom, but also let us use many of her best stories from her years on the road.

Kim Conner, who keeps Casey sane and happy every day, and who patiently and enthusiastically supported our work on this book.

Sharon Myers, without whom Consulting Stance might not even exist and who diligently read and edited the final edition. Any mistakes in this version were added after she completed her final edits.

Biju George, who originally and ultimately made consulting interesting for Casey. In other words, "he showed me the fun in it." He's also the model for our Perfect Consultant. B - thank you, and let me know next time it's Friday, and you don't have stuff to do.

Brad Thompson, for being a mentor and a friend, and for providing critical feedback from his years as a consultant and one who helps consultants grow.

Jeff Hook and Chuck Linn, who launched Christine's consulting career and taught her many valuable lessons about leadership, management, work/life balance and career planning.

Scott Elequin, who introduced us and then made it possible for us to work together.

Steven Haynes, for providing perspective from a young consultant and encouraging us that we were reaching our audience.

Max Solodky, whose enthusiasm came at the right time.

Kelli Klemm, who enthusiastically provided the fresh perspective of a new college graduate.

Marisa Allen, whose conclusions helped us finish the book right.

Our special thanks go out to Danielle Fifer, Deborah Rebisz, Sean Alcott, Denise Dailey, Karen Chisholm, who helped with content and editing.

We would also like to thank every consultant we have ever worked with. Many of the lessons in these pages came from you.

Christine Lambden and Casey Conner

Contents

What is Consulting Stance?

You and everyone around you make thousands of decisions every day. Many of these are conscious decisions, like what to eat for lunch, what color to paint the living room, M&Ms vs. Skittles, or whether to turn left or right at a stop sign.

Others are subconscious decisions or automatic reactions rooted in habit or routine, such as ordering your burger without onions, putting your car keys on the hook by the back door when you walk into the house, or saying "Bless you!" when someone sneezes.

Each of these behaviors starts out as a thoughtful decision based on experience and the given situation, but over time the need to think about them fades. Eventually, you just automatically react without thinking.

In addition, most people have a collection of axioms or catchphrases that they use as shortcuts for their longer thought processes. We don't all share the same ones, or attach the same importance to each one, but here are a few common examples:

"Work before play."

"Never yell at a volunteer."

"Don't trust people who tell you how honest they are."

"When in doubt, don't."

"A closed mouth gathers no foot."

An axiom doesn't have to include a decision-making process or instructions for your response. It simply works as a highly effective guide post; a reminder, sometimes based on lessons that life has left in your book of experience, of how past decisions or reactions have turned out well or poorly. These guideposts take up less space in your brain, and they contain nuggets of wisdom you need to react quickly and appropriately in a given situation. But where do these axioms come from?

> *Wisdom is based on experience and, unfortunately, experience usually comes from making mistakes.*

Wisdom is based on experience and, unfortunately, experience usually comes from making mistakes. It can take an entire career to accumulate all the wisdom and experience you need to become an extraordinary consultant, and how many of us are willing to wait that long?

So, you ask, can wisdom and experience be learned from a book?

No book or training course can replace a lifetime of experience, but the right training can definitely prevent having to learn everything by making mistakes. Our goal is to teach you the skills you need to respond quickly and effectively to many situations without taking too much time to think about your response.

The Discipline of Consulting

What do you do when you give good advice and the client refuses to follow it? Do you sulk and stubbornly continue to restate your case after the decision has been made? Do you lurk silently, waiting for your opportunity to say, "I told you so!" and gloat? Or do you roll up your sleeves and work hard to make the wrong decision turn out right so the client can smugly say, "See? I was right all along! But thanks for working so hard to make my idea work." (Hint: It's option three.)

As a consultant who specializes in a particular software application or business function, you will find yourself answering the same questions over and over. In many cases, once you find the right example or analogy to make your point, you'll have no trouble recycling it in future situations. You'll find some of our favorites scattered throughout this book.

For example, every time we went into a new client site to implement an order management system, one of the persistent questions was "Why can't the system prevent us from entering duplicate customer names?" The key in this situation is to find an answer that is more detailed than "Because I said so," and is still simple enough to be quickly understood and accepted.

One consultant we know answers with, "I once implemented this application at a company that makes embroidery machines for sale to retail stores all over the country. Their customer database had literally hundreds of Yarn Barns in it, and each one was a legitimate, separate customer." With this simple example, he stopped the whining about system shortcomings and moved the meeting forward to a discussion of ways to prevent duplicate customers in the business process instead. Genius.

In our workshops, we start by describing the perfect consultant...the guy who knows exactly what to do in every situation, always has perfect control of his travel schedule, never misses a deadline or a subtle conversational cue. One reason we do this is purely practical: we don't want anyone in the room to mistakenly think we are perfect ourselves, or worse, to think we are arrogant enough to believe we are perfect. You will quickly discover that people are much more open to your advice if you admit you don't know everything and reserve the right to be wrong...sometimes.

We study perfection to give us a guide when we are trying to make a decision or choose the best response to a situation, not because we expect ourselves to be perfect. Remember, we are shooting for "extraordinary", not "perfect."

The best, most effective, most popular, highest-priced consultant we've ever worked with describes his success by saying that he:

- Gets stuff done

- Makes everyone happy

- Finds more billable work

We think this is a good summary of the critical success factors for extraordinary consulting. And believe it or not, getting stuff done is not the most important priority.

No one expects you to be a perfect consultant, but it helps to know what you are measuring against. If the perfect consultant knows all the answers and you don't, for instance, how are you going to deal with that? You've got to know in advance that you are going to say, "I don't know, but I'll find out," when someone asks a question to which you don't know the answer.

Suppose the perfect consultant is oblivious to corporate politics but you rather enjoy the occasional gossip campaign or conspiracy theory? You need to make a conscious decision to step out of your role as consultant when you get involved in a controversy or take sides in a turf war.

If the perfect consultant is discreet and you like to tell tales about your previous clients, at least acknowledge to your audience that you are breaking a golden rule of consulting.

We have identified the following characteristics of a perfect consultant. This is not a complete list, obviously, but it is a good indicator of the challenges we all face in trying to live up to this standard.

A perfect consultant is:

- Experienced in the role assigned

- Knowledgeable in the specific technology or business function

- Respectful of client culture and protocols

- Informed about client's business and market

- Mindful of client/project goals and objectives

- Effective as a liaison between warring departments

- Responsible with billing hours, expenses and resources

- Diligent with communication, reporting and documentation

Sounds impossible, right? No one can reasonably expect to always be perfect and still be human.

The key is mental preparation. Just as a martial arts student starts with learning the basic moves and practices them over and over until they are automatic responses, you can learn and practice basic behaviors that provide the solid footing, position and attitude that you want as a consultant.

Once you have learned the basic moves, you can combine them in complex combinations. In martial arts, these combinations of moves are called "forms", and it is in learning and mastering the forms that winners are created.

Just as a trained fighter walks through life with the confidence that he (or she) can conquer virtually any opponent, you will approach every consulting engagement with confidence that you already know exactly how to respond to any situation. In other words, you'll know that you can get into your *consulting stance* instantly, if needed.

We have a friend who is a martial arts champion. He is always thinking 27 moves ahead and knows exactly how he will respond to any given move on his opponent's part. For him, there are no surprises. Can you imagine his confidence going into a contest? Our goal is to train you to start thinking several moves ahead by anticipating your client's needs and requests, and to build the confidence to know that you can respond quickly and appropriately.

A consultant must build a strong foundation of basic skills, eventually putting them all together to become a "master" in their field.

Consulting Stance uses this basic martial arts analogy as an organizing principle for our seminars, and we have structured this book in the same way. A consultant must build a strong foundation of basic skills, eventually putting them all together to become a

14

"master" in their field.

As a consultant, you will face many challenges and opportunities. Every task and every interaction with your client is an opportunity to build the relationship and your reputation, and in every opportunity is the possibility of damage. With the right preparation and a few nuggets of wisdom, you can approach those interactions with Chuck Norris confidence and easily handle every challenge.

Whether you are about to finish college and are selecting a career, or you are in the twilight of doing your time on the proverbial corporate gerbil wheel, you are reading this book because you want to learn the foundational skills of consulting, to present yourself as frighteningly competent so as to compete effectively, to predict the moves you will need to make to survive and thrive, to handle the tools of the trade, to get into...Consulting Stance.

Who are we?

This is not a case of "if you can't do, teach". Between us, we have over thirty years of experience as consultants and as managers of teams of consultants. During most of that time, we were also working as consultants, living in hotels and logging thousands of airline miles.

We have both spent much of our careers training, coaching and mentoring consultants, first as peers and then as project leads and managers. We each have particular areas of expertise. Casey understands the technology and can read a balance sheet. Christine is good at negotiating and can remember what every single person cares about, though Casey is better at using that knowledge to make sure they are happy.

If you take each of our best qualities and put them together, we add up to the consultant you will be when you've been doing this for twenty or thirty years.

Grammar, Political Correctness and Other Considerations

We both shy away from the idea of overwhelming, intentional political correctness. We hope never to offend anyone, not because it's politically correct, but rather because we want to be kind, fair and truthful in all of our communication.

If your standard for communication requires that you be kind, hopefully you are holding yourself to a higher standard than being merely politically correct. If you give up truthfulness in favor of political correctness, you are not actually showing respect. Just the opposite.

Trying to follow arbitrary rules for political correctness is frustrating, particularly when it means you might accidentally offend someone who otherwise would have nothing against you. As an example, we tried to write the following sentence with political correctness and this is what we got:

"A consultant quickly realizes that he or she is responsible only to himself or herself and cannot let his or her manager be the final authority on ethical behavior."

After several sentences in a row that sounded equally convoluted, we consulted a grammar authority. We discovered that there are two commonly accepted alternatives. The first is contemporary, gender-neutral and politically correct:

"A consultant quickly realizes that one is responsible only to oneself and cannot let one's manager be the final authority on ethical behavior."

While less confusing to read, it sounds a little pompous and contrived, doesn't it? In fact, it sounds like we disapprove and are trying to gently distance ourselves from the subject. (If it doesn't sound that way to you, try saying it with a Monty Python accent.)

The other alternative offered by Strunk & White in <u>The Elements of Style</u>, the accepted authority on American-English grammar, is more traditional and was accepted as gender-neutral until the same year that "politically correct" was added to the encyclopedia. This version is:

"A consultant quickly realizes that he is responsible only to himself and cannot let his manager be the final authority on ethical behavior."

We tried all three methods on a variety of sentences and, after much soul-searching and debate, we've elected to use him-himself with the intention of evoking a gender-neutral impression, except where specifically stated otherwise. If this or any other reference offends a single reader, we offer our sincere apology and regret. (Now get over it.) As a male-female writing team and long-term professionals in the consulting industry, we consider the ability to succeed in consulting to be gender neutral as well.

We've tried to write in the same informal, conversational style we use in our classroom sessions. However, in the classroom, we often talk over each other, present differing points of view and generally act like old friends act at work. This would create unnecessary confusion in written form, so for the purposes of this book, we have agreed to a single opinion on each issue and have written as one voice, though we continue to use "we" because neither one of us wants to take all the credit (or blame). Also, it will make it harder for you to determine which story goes with which client, even if you manage to get your hands on our resumes. (It's not that hard, both our resumes are available online at www.consultingstance.com.)

One other thing. We've used a lot of contractions and parentheses. We'd like to avoid them, but we're going for an informal feel here. We think it's great, so we're hoping you'll enjoy it. (Excessive use of contractions in these sentences is intentional.)

Code Names and Secret Handshakes

We said earlier that a consultant must be discreet. We have a whole section later in the book dedicated to ethics, proprietary information, non-disclosure agreements and client confidentiality. But even though you have an obligation to protect your clients, you will also feel an irresistible urge to talk about them. In airports and restaurants and hotel lobbies, all the places that consultants gather, conversation about current and past client behaviors is common.

One consultant we know has developed a system that allows him to conduct business meetings in restaurants and to participate in information-sharing (a.k.a. "the gossip machine") without fear of betraying his customer. We have adopted his system for all our daily activities, and use it to share our war stories in training sessions and this book. We refer to all our client companies, past and present, as Biggish Inc. or just Biggish, for short.

If you were to sit in front of us on an airplane, you could listen to an entire three-hour conversation about the challenges and insane politics at our current client site, and you would never once hear either of us say the name of the company. You might be tempted to Google "Biggish" when you get home to see who we were talking about, but that wouldn't bring you any closer to an answer. (No, that wasn't code. Neither of us has ever done any work for Google. We'd like to, though. We hear those guys are awesome.)

At more than one site, we've taken it a step further and assigned code names to some of the key players. On one project, the IT Director we reported to was at the center of a political firestorm and we were constantly, legitimately paranoid that our lunch meetings and hallway conversations might be overheard.

The client in question had an unusual name and if someone heard it mentioned, they could have no doubt who we were talking about, even if they didn't recognize us at all. She was also a very tall, elegant, professional woman, not unlike the character played by Alison Janney on The West Wing, so we called her "Alison". Another controversial key player in the same political mess was a very down-to-earth, aw-shucks-ma'am guy who reminded us of Toby Keith, so we called him "Toby".

There are several rules about creating code names for people or companies:

- The code name cannot be too obvious or it's not really a code.

- It cannot be mean-spirited. If it's not an obvious compliment, at least be sure it's appropriate.

- You must be absolutely certain that the people in question would also see it as either a compliment or a legitimately funny joke, should they hear about it.

The last rule is the trickiest, but it also the most important. Never, ever assign a code name like "Attila" or "Cujo" to a customer. Or anybody, really. This will come back to bite you.

If your code names are used by more than one or two other people, you will not be able to control who hears about them. Sooner or later, someone will tell your client that you refer to their company as "Disaster Central" and you'll be out of a job before the day is over.

Purpose of This Book

This book is intended to stand alone as a guide for new consultants, or to accompany classroom or group study workshops. If you can't have us come to your office and conduct our workshops, which would be the best way to get hands-on practice with the principles in this book, we hope to provide an acceptable substitute here.

We encourage consulting managers to use this as a guide and incorporate their own experience and war stories into their presentations. Our training materials are mostly adapted from presentations we created for our clients or for our own internal use, and several of the chapters in this text were originally written as white papers to be presented at various conferences.

We focused our examples and discussion on IT projects, particularly complex application implementations. This is where we gained our experience, so this is what we know best. Most of the actual wisdom in these pages would apply to any consulting engagement, so we've tried to include only the information that is necessary to understand the message and eliminated as much technical jargon as possible.

A Word About Sources

Our workshop sessions are filled with tales from our past and we have reproduced all of those stories as accurately as possible in these pages. We have suppressed all company names and changed the names of specific individuals we encountered (to avoid legal hassles) but the changes do not detract from the lessons.

If you have stories that might also illustrate our points, or if you have a nugget of wisdom that you'd like to share, you can email us at wisdom@consultingstance.com. If we like your story, we might include it (with credit to you) in our next edition. You can also post it on our Tales From The Road blog.

ℰ❦ ❧

Now that you know who we are, we can jump directly into the basic moves and tactics that will give you the edge as a consultant. Each of these "basic move" concepts seems simple at first, but the key is to master each one so that you do it without thinking every time it's appropriate. Recognize when you are tempted to guess and *ask* the question instead. *Listen* intently when someone else is talking, in every single conversation, rather than letting your mind wander.

One of the best ways to develop these habits is to work with a partner or team using this common vocabulary to help your communication. If you are working side-by-side with someone who is also trying to master these moves, you can help each other. For instance, if you are dawdling in the hallway when you are supposed to be walking into a meeting, your partner can say, "Don't forget...*easy stuff*!" and you'll remember that you have decided to do the easy stuff perfectly. With his help, you'll get to your meeting on time, even though you had a temporary lapse of discipline.

We have grouped the basic moves into four categories: Fundamental Moves, Communication Moves, Integrity Moves and Administrative Moves.

Fundamental Moves

People come into consulting from a variety of situations. It is common for consulting firms to recruit people who have the necessary technical or business skills from "regular jobs". For instance, one of the best consultants we know, Tony, started out driving the forklift in a warehouse. When his company decided to implement an enterprise-wide computer system, Tony was assigned to the IT project to represent the warehouse primarily because he could easily be spared from his usual role for a few months. Also, he was very young, smart, and interested in computers.

After participating on the project team, his knowledge of the system made him more valuable to IT than to the warehouse staff, so he was moved into a business analyst role in IT. After a few years of solving problems and answering users' questions, his knowledge had expanded to include the entire corporate system and he had, along the way, developed a talent for listening to a user, understanding his problem, and then finding a solution quickly. They loved him.

Eventually, he was assigned to another project team where he worked with consultants from a large firm who were impressed by his knowledge of the system and his understanding of the day-to-day challenges faced by the users. A few months later, when his company was purchased and his entire department eliminated, he remembered those consultants and contacted them in hopes of getting a job referral. His reasoning was that they must know lots of companies who need people like him.

He was right.

They hired him immediately and now he travels all over the country working with users and systems, advising senior managers about their business processes and systems. We personally know of at least three other consulting firms who would jump at the chance to steal him away from his current employer, which is the best job security in the world.

When Tony first moved from his familiar IT role into consulting, he thought it would be a much easier transition than the one he made so many years ago from kid-in-the-warehouse to IT-analyst-with-no-experience-whatsoever, but he was surprised by how much of the IT consulting role actually has nothing to do with computers or even users. As we said, he quickly became a superstar, but not before learning the fundamentals of consulting that have nothing to do with the actual work and everything to do with setting yourself up to be successful in that work.

The Fundamental Moves are:

- *Get full value from every "first day"* on a new project or at a new client site.

- Learn to think ahead. The goal is to be able to predict what will happen *27 moves* in advance.

- Always try to *do the easy stuff perfectly*.

- *Pick your battles*. Not every difference of opinion is worth going to battle over and not every battle is worth winning.

- *There are politics in results*. Sometimes it isn't enough to solve the problem, you have to be sure you communicate that you solved the problem correctly.

- *Consulting can mean you have a very long commute*. Working in other cities is exciting, but it's also hard. There are ways to make it easier for yourself.

- And above all, *get along with everyone* you meet.

This section describes each of these moves. They are the core foundation on which you'll build your consulting career.

Get Full Value From Every First Day

The first day on a new consulting engagement or project is very important. You may get away with being dressed wrong, showing up late and having no idea what the project is all about, because "It's my first day." However, in the spirit of thinking ahead, you should have clarified the logistical issues before showing up at your client. In consulting, the honeymoon period is very short, and to quote an overused proverb, you never get a second chance to make a good first impression. That being said, after the first day, you will be expected to be productive and to fit into the environment.

Here are some guidelines and tips for getting started on a consulting engagement. Use your time wisely on the first day to learn what you need to know.

Follow the dress code. If possible, dress one step above it, unless that will offend people at this client site. Sometimes it does. Ask. If you are unsure how to do this, consult a professional to help with your image. They really can help you eliminate distracting elements in your wardrobe and make you seem more confident and credible.

Make friends with the guard or receptionist on the first day. A smile now will definitely pay off later.

Learn the client's and project team's expectations about working arrangements. On some projects, traveling consultants are expected to fly home on Thursday evening. On others, taking a full hour for lunch is considered wasteful and self-indulgent.

Make friends with the guard or receptionist on the first day. A smile now will definitely pay off later. Ditto for the client's

25

administrative assistant, who shall not be called "hey you" or "ma'am"...she has a name and a family and a story – learn them.

Don't park in the Visitor Parking unless specifically instructed to. The best spaces are reserved for customers, not consultants.

Accept kindness from new clients and contacts. If your contact starts by offering you coffee, accept. He might not remember again, and you'll want to know where stuff is. You don't have to drink it, or even take some, once you are in the break room. You can change your mind to have a soda or a bottle of water.

Don't start with a complaint about traffic, location or parking. Nobody likes a whiner, and your clients may have driven further than you did.

Bring something with you to discreetly entertain yourself, as the first week or so may involve a lot of waiting. Hooking up your Wii to the TV in the break room is not discreet, nor is playing solitaire with real cards. Your best bet is the internet, but you should limit yourself to news sites, industry-related sites, or reading white papers about topics in your field.

Write down names. Be sure to bring at least a pen and paper to take notes. Unless you are gifted with a memory for people's names, you will want to write down the names of people you meet.

It isn't necessary to write down the names of every single person who is mentioned on your first day, but it is extremely important to learn the names of the key people on your project and in your business unit. If possible, write down the names of everyone you meet in your first week, along with something meaningful (and flattering) about them. It should be flattering because they'll probably read it either as you write it or months later when you can't possibly remember why you wrote "jerk", "mole-icious" or "nice hair piece!" in your notebook next to the name.

Carry business cards that have your cell phone and email addresses printed. You'll need to tell people how to reach you before you are in the client's email directory. Also, write your name and cell phone number on the inside of your notebook. You will lose it eventually and you'll want the person who finds it to be able to return it to you.

Be flexible with your work hours. If a key user in your business unit works from 6 a.m. to 2 p.m., be prepared to work the same hours. Don't worry. Most likely he works those hours to get some peace and quiet in the morning. He won't want you there at 6 a.m. every day for long.

Here is a partial list of information you should be sure to collect on the first day (or as soon as possible):

- Who directs my work?

- What are my specific responsibilities?

- Who approves my work schedule and priorities?

- Does overtime require pre-approval?

- Who do I ask when I'm not sure whether to escalate an issue?

- What is the scope of this project? Is there a detailed contract or Statement of Work that I should be familiar with?

- Where is the project in relation to the timeline?

- What do I own?

- How important are deadlines?

- What's the dress code and how important is it?

- How much time can we really ask and get from the employees?

- How late do people really work? When do they show up?

- Is it okay to bring coffee into meetings?

- Do meetings start on time?

- Who will show up and who won't?

- What's the best way to ensure participation?

- Who's the one who really gets things done?

- What's the name of the "IT guy" who can help us with all our connectivity and network problems?

- Are people picky about deliverable formats, or does "quick and dirty" work?

- Does the client appreciate it when Dilbert cartoons and posters from Despair.com are included in presentations?

This list is just to get you started and give you an idea of the sort of questions you should be asking. We could go on and on. As you progress in your career, you'll add questions to this list based on your own experience.

Think 27 Moves Ahead

Remember the martial arts expert we told you about in the first chapter? He is always thinking 27 moves ahead. He knows exactly what he is going to do and every possible response his opponent might deliver. His next move might change as a result of his opponent's action, but the overall trajectory of the contest is clear in his mind at all times.

It takes years of practice and study to reach that level, both in martial arts and in consulting. But in both disciplines, you have to start with this objective in mind. Even if you are only thinking ahead one or two moves, you are going to be better prepared and more effective than if you are not.

Practice thinking ahead.

Even if you don't have the experience and instincts to predict 27 events into the future, you can look ahead on your calendar and identify tasks that could be done prior to upcoming meetings or deadlines. For instance, if you have a meeting with key users on Thursday, send an email on Wednesday to remind them of your agenda so they are able to bring the necessary data, answers or experts to the meeting.

Cultivate the ability to plan and predict. People may start to think you are psychic.

Look at the whole project plan and see what emergencies might be coming your way. If you're a business analyst and you see that the developers are starting to test their code next week, you can predict that they are going to ask you for some sample data. Get it ready ahead of time so their last-minute request does not create a crisis for you. If you are the developer, think about what you might need next week and ask the business analysts for their sample data in advance.

Look at the Steering Committee calendar. If the next meeting is on Monday, you might predict that the Project Manager is going to ask for a new update to the slide he uses to report status on your part of the project. Get it ready ahead of time.

The practical application of "27 Moves" can even be as simple as checking the weather and leaving for work 20 minutes early on the days when it's raining. Unless you live in a city where rain does not adversely affect traffic, this is always a good idea. (If you live in a city where rain does not affect traffic, please send an email to info@consultingstance.com because we would like to move our corporate headquarters there immediately.)

Cultivate the ability to plan and predict. People may start to think you are psychic.

"Unintended Consequences"

Part of thinking 27 moves ahead is being prepared for any number of possible responses to a given move, which means you have to consider not only the best-case response, but also other probable responses, the unlikely response and the extremely unlikely response. It ALSO means you have to be prepared for additional consequences that aren't directly related to your move-countermove plan. This is where unintended consequences come in.

Unintended consequences are things that happen as a direct result of your actions that were not predicted and for which no contingency plan is in place. For instance, if a dedicated coffee drinker gives up caffeine, he might expect to feel sleepy in the morning. If this causes him to be late to work three days in a row, getting into trouble with his boss is an unintended consequence of giving up caffeine.

If you wash your car and then it rains, this is not an unintended consequence. No matter how much you think the two are connected, there is no cause-effect relationship between clean cars and rain.

If a company implements a new accounting solution that will automate many transactions, their goal may be to cut costs and reduce headcount. In this situation, the resulting layoff of employees is not an unintended consequence, since it was expected. If the same accounting implementation also results in more accurate revenue recognition and the company is required to restate earnings for the past four quarters, the resulting SEC investigation would be an unintended consequence.

Predicting unintended consequences will enhance your effectiveness as a consultant. Predicting them 27 moves ahead and allowing time to change course or prepare for catastrophe is our goal.

Do the Easy Stuff Perfectly

Every consulting practice has one or two superstars who can get away with ignoring deadlines and breaking rules. These guys are so consistently brilliant with sales or client relationships that the practice manager or project manager is forced to tolerate their disrespect for policy. If you are one of these people, we see that silly grin on your face. If you know one of these people, we feel your pain!

Here's what you may not know: management may be forced to tolerate the behavior for a while, but they do not like it. If they find an occasionally brilliant, disciplined replacement who will submit status reports on time and show up for meetings, the superstar is history. There is more job security and long-term success in doing the easy stuff perfectly and being occasionally brilliant. [Note: This is very good news for us.]

Learn how to manage your calendar and to-do list so that you remember when things are due and have ample time to do them early.

Learn how to manage your calendar and to-do list so that you remember when things are due and have ample time to do them early. For example, if status reports are due on Tuesday by 5pm, set aside an hour on Monday afternoon to prepare the report. Early Tuesday afternoon, review the report you prepared and make changes, if needed, based on what has happened in the last 24 hours. Submit it early.

Manage your inter-meeting commute. If you are scheduled to be in a meeting in another building at 2:30, add an appointment on your calendar at 2:15 to give you time to walk over.

Answer your email. Email has replaced phone calls in most companies for efficient communication. E-mail can be good because it allows the sender to write whenever he has available time, and you may answer when you have time. A phone call requires that you both be available at the same time, often resulting in a frustrating game of Phone Tag or, worse, the "increasingly long, over-explanatory voice mail" game. However, the advantage of email for quick, convenient communication is completely lost if you allow your inbox to fill up and do not read and respond to incoming messages quickly. Stay current on reading and responding to email.

Stay current on reading and responding to email.

As a consultant, you have higher visibility than the average employee, for many reasons. You need to be conscious of who and how many people are watching you, even if you are working in a computer lab and never see users or upper management. They usually know who you are, and if they don't, it's often good to keep it that way.

Be sensitive to your client's competition. If you are working at Dell, don't bring an HP laptop. If you are working at Freescale, try to bring a Motorola phone. If you don't know why you need a Motorola phone at Freescale, you didn't do enough homework on who your client is and why they might care.

For goodness sake, if you're working at Hershey, don't break out a Nestle Crunch bar!

This is Easy Stuff. Do it perfectly.

Pick Your Battles

Very early in our relationship with Biggish, we found ourselves in a meeting where representatives from another consulting firm were presenting their recommendations to senior management to solve a major procurement issue. Their proposal was to build a massive, custom system to perform critical purchasing functions. The system would cost Biggish at least $10 million, but the obvious return-on-investment was much larger, so the proposal was likely to be accepted.

We were in the meeting simply to learn the details of the proposal so that our project, which involved a totally separate system and different procurement activities, could accommodate the proposed changes in data.

Throughout the two-hour meeting, we listened to the other firm as they reviewed the system requirements, described the proposed solution and defined all the business process and architecture changes that would be required. Furthermore, their plan would take two years to complete.

Not all issues are equal. Don't fight every battle. You'll be exhausted in the first two weeks, and you'll embarrass yourself by choosing a battle that, as you learn later, isn't really worth fighting.

About halfway through the meeting, we began to realize that there was a flaw in their assumptions. The packaged application that we had been hired to implement could meet all of the requirements they had identified and had already been purchased. In fact, we were scheduled to deliver the system into production within six months, and could easily make the few configuration changes needed to combine the two project's objectives.

More importantly, it was clear from the presentation materials that the other consulting firm was aware of our project and had access to information about the capabilities of our system.

We had a clear obligation to tell our client that the proposed project was unnecessary. The challenge was to decide when and how to present the information. If we interrupted the meeting to contradict the rival firm's conclusions publicly, our egos would have been satisfied, but we would have earned ourselves at least one enemy at the client site. No one likes to be proven wrong, but embarrassing our competition in front of our mutual customer would have been a mistake.

Instead of going to battle in front of the client, we elected to meet privately with the other firm after the meeting. We warned them that we would have to tell our client that the packaged software they had already purchased could do everything the proposed system would do, with a much smaller price tag and time commitment. We gave them an opportunity to revise their recommendations themselves, which they did. Out of gratitude for our discreet handling of the situation, they also gave us full credit for identifying the alternative solution and we gained allies inside the client company and our competitor's organization.

In a different situation at a different client site, the customer asked us to design an auxiliary system for their financial applications that would effectively create a false audit trail to support manually altered transactions. After the initial discovery sessions, we realized that we could not in good conscience build the system they wanted. (If you don't understand why not, refer to the chapter on Ethics in this book or Google "Enron".)

Furthermore, we decided that the Finance staff members involved honestly did not realize that what they were suggesting was unethical. We began by very, very politely suggesting that the auditors might have some objections to the proposed plan. When that argument did not work, we were forced to state our position more clearly. "You cannot do this. You will get in trouble. And if we help you, we will get in trouble, too."

We try to evaluate each situation based on whether it violates our ego or our ethics. If someone at the client site accuses us of making a mistake or showing poor judgment, we often decide it is not a battle worth fighting. If we are asked to violate the law or our ethics, we fight. Most problems fall somewhere in between.

Not all issues are equal. Don't fight every battle. You'll be exhausted in the first two weeks, and you'll embarrass yourself by choosing a battle that, as you learn later, isn't really worth fighting.

The Politics of Results

Bill Clinton, regardless of what you think of his politics or personal life, has been wildly successful throughout his career at getting things done and making people like him. Political analysts and pundits have studied his methods to find the secret of his success, but it only takes one conversation with him to discover the key. He listens carefully, asks questions designed to elicit details, and responds to what you care about.

If your approval rating drops below a certain (unofficial) percentage with your customer, your ability to advise them is limited and the likelihood of your success diminishes.

During campaigns, his associates often complained about his unwillingness to stick to scripted "talking points" during casual conversations with voters. Instead, he would cling to whichever topic most concerned the other person in the conversation, ignoring his own agenda until he was sure they knew they had been heard and answered. It was a successful strategy. Clinton was elected Governor of Arkansas six times and President of the United States twice.

Consultants also have to manage their popularity. If your approval rating drops below a certain (unofficial) percentage with your customer, your ability to advise them is limited and the likelihood of your success diminishes.

You may be thinking, "I shouldn't have to schmooze my customer. They should like me because I know what I'm talking about. They should listen and trust me because of my experience." You are right, but your job will be easier if you learn to manage the politics of relationships and results.

Bob, who is an IT consultant, recently had an opportunity to do this. He was sitting in a conference room before the meeting started when a user he knew only slightly walked in and plopped down in her chair with a big sigh.

"How's it going?" he asked. Already you see his political savvy at work...he spoke to her instead of continuing to read email on his laptop.

"Awful. The [insert financial report name here] report won't balance and I can't find the problem. I have to get it fixed today and I do not have time for this meeting!"

Bob neatly avoided two common consulting traps with his response. He did not say, "It's too bad that is outside my scope or I could probably help you," and he did not list a dozen obvious things she could try in a condescending voice using technical jargon she wouldn't understand. Instead, he said, "Sometimes a second pair of eyes can help. Would you like me to sit down with you after this meeting and we can take a look?"

Notice that Bob didn't promise that he would solve the problem, nor did he promise to dedicate the rest of his already-packed day to it, but he responded to her concern with a practical offer to help.

After the meeting, she took him up on his offer. They went through the report together and Bob was, luckily, able to find and resolve the issue quickly. The customer was grateful and said so.

At this point, Bob had already demonstrated his value as a consultant. To manage his client's perception of the exchange, he said, "I'm glad I could help. That's what I'm here for."

It isn't necessary to hammer the point home. Most people are uncomfortable with bragging or making every conversation a sales pitch. A gentle reminder that having a consultant around is helpful will enhance your perceived value. Your actual value depends on *actually* being able to help.

Follow these steps to increase your perceived value:

1. Listen carefully to be sure you understand the issue.

2. Help resolve the issue.

3. When the customer says thank you, say, "Just doing my job. I'm a consultant. That's how we roll."

The Really Long Commute

Travel is a fact of life for most consultants. Many spend 45 weeks on the road every year, and some say they wouldn't want it any other way.

We know one married couple where both are traveling consultants. They often joke that they should write a book called "Marriage on Three Days a Week" because they only see each other from Thursday night to Sunday night most weeks. Of course, they take great vacations with all the frequent flier miles and hotel points, and neither one is left at home to manage the household while the other dines in restaurants every night and comes home expecting all the chores to be done.

Take steps to create an environment on the road that is as close to your environment at home as possible. Familiar surroundings make travel easier.

Like many others, they have learned how to be comfortable on the road so that their travel schedules are a source of new experiences and great stories instead of a hardship. If you learn how to be comfortable in your environment, you'll do better work and last longer in this demanding field.

There are two types of IT consulting roles, from a travel schedule perspective. One type of consultant is the real Road Warrior who is in a different city each week, often visiting two or three different clients and staying only a couple of days each place. The other type travels to the same destination every week to work on a long-term engagement over several months. Which type of travel schedule you end up with depends as much on your personality as on your skill set.

No matter which type of travel schedule you have, there are some seemingly small things you can do to make yourself significantly more comfortable on the road.

Enroll in every frequent flier and hotel points program you can. The biggest perks in business travel come when you get a free family vacation later. All those trips to Pittsburgh might buy you a trip to Honolulu or Prague or wherever your heart leads you.

Whenever possible, use the same airline and hotel chain for every city. This helps you rack up the points faster, and it also establishes a level of comfort and familiarity for you from the moment you arrive in the city. Not every Marriott is exactly like every other Marriott, but there are enough similarities between them that you will begin to feel at home quickly.

Packing for Travel

Develop a routine for packing. Make a checklist that includes everything that you know you'll need for any trip, including items like toothbrush and cell-phone charger. Go over the checklist every single time you pack a suitcase.

If you don't follow this advice, you will eventually end up spending $200 on a "charge everything" device and using a hotel toothbrush that will rip your gums out.

1. Always assume you will have to carry your luggage yourself. If you aren't sure you will need it, don't take it. You can always buy one there. (Don't accept engagements in locations that don't have stores.)

2. Pack something comfortable to wear in your hotel room and clothes you can wear to work out.

3. Plan to sleep in something you don't mind being seen wearing in public. In the event of a fire, hotels will evacuate two floors

above and two floors below, even if it's just a small fire in a trash basket. That's what that loudspeaker above the bed is for.

4. All luggage looks alike. Make your bag easy to spot on the carousel and less likely to be stolen with a few strategically placed strips of duct tape or a big pink bow.

5. The military knows that rolled clothing does not wrinkle. Don't fold it, roll it. Turn jackets inside out, fold the collar up and press one shoulder inside the other.

6. Think about what you pack from the perspective of Customs and Airport Security. For example, many airlines will not allow you to carry steel-tipped darts in your carry-on luggage. (Yes, one of us learned this the hard way. Not the one you think.) Carry all medication in the original packages, particularly prescription medication.

7. Purchase two of everything you use daily, like cosmetics, razors, toothbrush, etc. Leave one set at home. Pack toiletries once and leave them packed. This way, you don't have to worry that you forgot something essential and will not notice until the middle of the night in a strange hotel room. When you run out of something on the road, replace it. (This is easier if you use common brands that are sold nationally.)

After only a few weeks of travel, you'll know exactly what you need to pack and what you don't.

Hotel Living

If you are traveling to the same city every week, pick a hotel that you are comfortable in and make friends with the people at the front desk and in Housekeeping. If you can commit to a certain number of weeks, they might even give you a break on the room rate, which is also good for your customer.

Once you've tried two or three different rooms in different parts of the hotel, you'll begin to identify specific things you like or dislike. Within a few weeks, you'll probably have a favorite room. Don't be afraid to ask for it every week. Staying in the same room every week can increase your sense of comfort and it's easier to remember what room you are in. Every one of us has been frustrated at least once by trying to open a hotel room door, only to realize that the key doesn't work because this is the room we were in last week, and we have no idea what room we have been assigned this week.

If you followed our instructions for packing and bought duplicates of all your toiletries and travel needs, you can check a suitcase with the bellman over the weekend instead of carrying it home with you. Leave your laundry with a dry cleaner over the weekend and come back on Monday to a fresh wardrobe without carrying a bag with you to the airport. That's freedom!

Make friends with the people who have control of the food. If you are eating all your meals off the Room Service menu, you will soon get bored with the choices. Encourage the person who answers the Room Service line to give you suggestions.

When Christine was working in one city where it wasn't considered safe to leave the hotel and wander around at night, she called the Room Service number one night and said, in the most pitiful voice she could muster, "I'm hungry and nothing on the menu looks good tonight. Help me!"

The Room Service voice laughed and said, "Miss Lambden, don't you worry. After all these months, I know what you like. Let me surprise you."

In addition to the best steak and the freshest salad ever served by Room Service, the waiter brought a glass of red wine and said, "The chef said to tell you that he knows you don't like red wine, but this is special. Try it with the steak. Alternate one bite of steak with one sip of wine."

She still talks about that steak. After that night, she never had to look at the Room Service menu again. When she called, she would say, "Maybe a fish tonight?" or "I'm in the mood for something chocolate."

Remember, if you are tired of the hotel menu, just imagine how the chef feels.

Since you can't eat all the time, here are some other ways to fill an evening in a hotel room:

1. Call your mother.

2. Read.

3. Go to a movie.

4. College libraries are often open till midnight. Learn something.

5. Work out. Remember the Freshman Fifteen in college? The life of a consultant includes too many meals in restaurants and too few long walks in the park.

If you exercise at home, try to exercise the same way when you are traveling. Find out if it's safe to walk/run outside near the hotel. This is also a great way to find the neighborhood restaurants and pubs that the travel books don't know about.

If you exercise in a gym at home, stay in a hotel with a gym and use it. If there is no gym available in the hotel, remember that many national chains have memberships that allow you to work out in any city. Like national hotel and restaurant chains, gyms are a great way to find familiar surroundings in an unfamiliar place.

Exploring new cities is a great way to get exercise and enjoy your time on the road. See the sights. Shop. Ask the people at the hotel and at work what you should be sure to see while you are in town.

We know one consultant who managed, in one year, to see Niagara Falls (working in Buffalo), the Arch in St. Louis, the Napa Valley wine country, six shows on Broadway, and Fort Lauderdale during Spring Break.

Did you know that Kansas City is the City of Fountains? In the winter, the city slowly freezes some of the fountains so you see frozen ice where water flows in the summer. Just beautiful.

Did you know that you can visit the Budweiser Clydesdales at Grant's Farm in St. Louis? If you think they are fun to watch on Super Bowl commercials, just imagine how magnificent they are up close.

These opportunities may not present themselves again. Don't spend every evening in your hotel room.

Every city has something unique to offer and the people who live there will be happy to help you discover what is wonderful about their hometown.

Single Life on the Road

The constant-travel lifestyle is often more appealing to single people who do not have a family at home waiting for them each week. For these consultants, the only challenge is finding a way to maintain a home when you aren't there during the week.

Here are some tips:

1. Ask a friend or neighbor to pick up your mail once or twice during the week.

2. Install automatic light timers in your house. Install motion sensor lights outside. This makes it look like someone is home and protects your stuff. (It also makes bats and possums find another yard to live in, but that might just be an Austin thing.)

3. Hide valuables. Burglars know all about looking in the freezer for your jewelry, but would they think to look in that bag of potting soil in the garage? Hint: Tell someone you trust where you hid them...you'll remember all the great spots you considered, and you'll forget the one you picked.

4. Splurge a little with all that money you are making as a consultant and hire a maid service to come in and clean your house while you are gone. If you have a lawn, hire a yard service, too. The last thing you are going to feel like doing when you finally get home is housework, and you'll be happier in this job if you don't feel that you are neglecting chores.

5. If possible, have a trusted house-sitter stay in your house. Then you won't have to worry at all.

In addition to maintaining your house, a single person on the road has to maintain a social life. When you are out of town all week, it's easy to find yourself excluded from your friends' conversations about plans for the weekend. You have to work harder to maintain those friendships at home, especially if you are also forming new friendships in the city where you are working.

It's not totally unheard of for consultants assigned to the same client week after week to form friendships, or even romantic attachments, in the city where they work. Having bonds with people all over the country can be a huge advantage professionally because your network is expanded to include all of their colleagues, as well.

Don't date someone in the client company. This can get messy. (Yeah, we know. Your situation is different. You'll handle it like grownups. We'd like to believe this, but in our experience it rarely works out that way. Even so, this is still good advice for everyone else.)

Married With Children

Life on the road is harder for those who have a family at home. You miss them and you feel guilty about leaving them behind, and even more guilty when you're having fun without them.

The same tourist attractions that enliven a single person's travel can make you miss your family even more. You find yourself thinking, "The kids would love this," or "Niagara Falls by myself? I don't think so!"

Here are some tips for making travel easier when you miss your family:

1. Write long letters saying all the stuff you would have said if you were at home. Buy a fax machine for the house so you can send them before you go to bed and the family can read them with breakfast. (We know. Email works just as well. Except it doesn't. Handwritten letters mean more. They just do.)

2. Give the hotel's fax number to your family or set up a personal e-fax number. Encourage letters from home. Also drawings and report cards and anything else that will make you feel closer. Almost all children could benefit from the occasional writing exercise, and most of them already know how to operate a computer.

3. Buy a small digital camera or use your cell phone to take pictures and make a "Day in the Life" slide show for the kids. Take pictures of your day from the time you wake up to the time you prepare for bed – pictures of your hotel room, your breakfast plate, your cubicle and co-workers, the bookstore you stop at after work, the restaurants you like – everything! (Trust us, they'll love it.)

Driving in Strange (translation: "New To You") Places

Weather conditions and driver courtesy rules vary from city to city. In some cities, driving is a brutal competition, and it's considered rude or suicidal to slow down for a yellow light. Someone will honk at you or run into you. In others, you'll get dirty looks if you don't yield and let a waiting car merge in front of you. On most country roads, failure to wave at passing drivers marks you as an outsider.

No matter where you are, these tips will help lessen the impact of driving during your travels:

1. Get a map when you arrive. If you know where you are going, you are much less likely to end up in the wrong place.

2. If you rear-end a car on the freeway, your first move should be to hang up the phone. Better yet, go hands-free when you are driving. Best of all, hang up and drive.

3. Rent your car from the same agency every week and be extra nice. Usually, the same agents are on duty every Monday morning, so eventually they'll know you and may offer you the cool convertible or the Jag for a week at no extra charge.

4. Not every state or city has a "right on red" law. Check with the car rental agency or look for a "No right on red" sign before you assume it's legal in any intersection where you are.

5. If you are stopped for speeding, running a red light, driving the wrong way, or, worst of all, hitting something, be very polite to everyone involved. Of course, this is true when you aren't traveling, too, but you have a better chance of making your meeting or flight if you deal with the situation nicely.

In New York or Boston (or London or Beijing), take a cab or public transportation. Some warnings say "Don't try this at home." With regard to driving in these places, the rule is "Don't try this on the road." In other words, ask someone at your destination or consult a travel guide to find out whether it's advisable to drive yourself around.

If you are facing your first winter in a snowy climate, ask someone to teach you how to drive in icy conditions before the first blizzard. You may feel foolish, and they will definitely laugh at you, but the first time you feel your car start to slide, you'll be glad you did.

For us, just saying "I'm from Texas" is often enough to have our clients offer free driving lessons, icy conditions or not.

Air Travel Tips

Since 9/11, keeping track of the rules for air travel and getting through Security checkpoints has become more of a challenge, but the airlines have made a sincere effort to help.

Every airline and airport website has information about security requirements and how much time will be required to get to your gate. Experienced travelers quickly learn to avoid the busiest times of the day and week. In fact, we don't know a single traveling consulting who would consider flying on the day before Thanksgiving, under any circumstances.

Airport websites will also give you information about other amenities that are available in the terminals. For instance, did you know that the Hong Kong airport has showers and rooms where you can take a nap? After a long flight across the Pacific ocean, a shower is a wonderful way to spend your three-hour layover between connecting flights.

The airport in Portland, Oregon, has a great mall. You can get all your Christmas shopping done between flights and have the items you bought shipped home. Oh, and did we mention that Oregon doesn't have sales tax?

The San Francisco airport has twenty different museum galleries that rotate art, culture and science exhibitions on a regular schedule. At SFO, you can't avoid being entertained and educated while you travel.

Here are some other tips for making air travel easier:

1. When you make your reservations, ask for a seat near the front of the plane. Airlines assign seats back-to-front and families traveling with children tend to plan further ahead than business travelers, so the shrieking three year-olds are usually in the back of the plane.

2. Always request the Exit Row. Children aren't permitted, and you get more legroom.

3. Wear earplugs or invest in some good noise-canceling headphones if you plan to sleep. People talk louder on airplanes.

4. Planes have only 3% humidity, so you get dehydrated quickly. Carry a bottle of water on board. (This will also keep your feet from swelling.) To keep costs and carryon weight low, carry an empty bottle and ask the flight attendant to fill it for you. On international flights, there is usually a water fountain available for passengers to serve themselves.

5. When they say, "Limit two carry-on bags," assume they really mean it and be prepared to check everything but your purse, briefcase and laptop. A good alternative if you are in a hurry is to "gate check" your bags. Especially with smaller commuter flights, this means you get your bags immediately when you get off the plane with no stop at baggage claim.

6. Pay attention to the safety speech every once in a while. Like washing your car to make it rain, it's just good karma. We've asked, and yes, most flight attendants feel just as silly giving the speech as you do listening to it, but the fact that no one is listening just makes their job harder.

7. To prevent a stiff neck from sleeping on a plane, ask the flight attendant for a blanket, roll it up and wrap it around your neck before you fall asleep. Your head won't roll from side-to-side, you won't snore and you won't look nearly as ridiculous as those people drooling on their neighbor's shoulder. They make C-shaped pillows that do this, but that's just one more thing to carry with you. We prefer to travel light.

While you are traveling, do everything you can to make your life easier. When you are enjoying yourself, you are better prepared to perform at work, and you'll be more successful.

Cubicles and conference rooms are the same everywhere. The work won't change, but taking the time to make friends with the people around you, at work and at the hotel, will make all the difference in the world to how well you do it.

Get Along With People

As we said before, one of the keys to a successful consulting career is the ability to make people happy. For you to achieve this, they have to like you. Being popular is not more important than being competent, but it is *as* important. You will get more done if people want to help you, if you listen to them and they listen to you, and if they are pleased when you succeed.

When you encounter someone new, don't hesitate to introduce yourself. Smile, say "Hello, my name is Bob Smith," and extend your right hand. Everyone, without exception, will smile at you, say their name and shake your hand. This is an important social ritual. So important, in fact, that there are people who teach classes in the proper way to shake hands and to remember names.

Pay attention when you first meet someone. Look directly at them and focus on the conversation for a moment, no matter how large the group or how busy you are. We worked with one ambitious Director who had mastered the genuine-looking smile and handshake, and who introduced himself eagerly every time he encountered us. The first time, we were impressed by his professionalism and sincere pleasure at finally meeting us. The second time, we understood that he is very busy and meets a lot of people, so our appreciation was not diminished. The fifth time he introduced himself to us, we knew without a doubt that he was not even aware of our presence in the conversation.

You will get more done if people want to help you, if you listen to them and they listen to you, and if they are pleased when you succeed.

He was operating on auto-pilot. It became a joke, which was not at all the impression he wanted to create.

Here are more general guidelines that will help you, no matter what job you are in:

- Give away information. Part of your value to the client and to your colleagues is the information you bring.

- Share credit for accomplishments with the people who participated.

- Offer sincere praise to colleagues.

- Volunteer for *a few* unpopular jobs or tasks.

- Be punctual.

- Smile.

- Be upbeat and optimistic.

- Be someone others can, and do, count on.

- Never criticize how someone else handles a problem. No one appreciates a back seat driver.

- If the team goes to lunch, go sometimes. Don't be the guy who always eats at his desk.

- Come early. Stay late. Set a good first impression of being a hard worker. It buys goodwill later.

- Turn off your cell phone ringer. Leave the room to take calls.

Toxic Topics

We compiled the following list of conversation topics to avoid. In any group of people, you will find that some of these topics are perfectly acceptable and that there are others that unexpectedly wreak havoc in the atmosphere. Start with these, but use your own judgment about which conversations to join and which to abandon. Remember that one of your critical success factors is getting along with people.

- Politics

- Religion

- Money

- Sex

- Capital punishment

- Other races, religions or cultures (the most innocent statements can sound critical)

- How previous projects were better

- How previous clients were smarter

- How many mistakes were made before you arrived

- How dumb the decisions were that got your client to this point

- How much you don't like the city you are working in

- How much you hate to travel

- Bill rates

- Pay rates

- Contract terms

These topics rarely make people like you; they are more likely to make them challenge/question your beliefs, your knowledge, your articulation, etc. You can only lose respect in these conversations, not gain it, unless you happen to totally agree. (And where is the fun in that?) Even then, at work most people will not admit to taking a side in a controversial topic when other people are around. Do not assume that the opinions people express in conversation at the office are their real opinions.

Don't Be That Guy!

We were on a project once where the project team members were all assigned cubicles on one floor of a huge building, which is a very common situation. What made this project special was that everyone on the team was usually focused intently on their work so it was very, very quiet on this floor. Cell-phone conversations took place in conference rooms and stairwells.

Sounds like heaven, right? Wrong.

Someone was humming. Very quietly. All day, every day. Most team members were able to ignore it. Some didn't even notice it. But for a few of us, this was an extremely irritating working situation.

It took us a few days to track down the source of the noise, and a few more days to decide how to address it. The culprit was a really nice guy who played in a band on the weekends. He may not have even known he was humming, and he certainly had no idea that he could be heard three rows away.

We finally ended up asking him, very good-naturedly, to either hum louder or not at all. And we warned him that if he picked louder, he would have to hum songs we knew, so we could sing along.

He took it well and the problem went away, but he still made our List Of Annoying People To Work With, because...well, it was seriously annoying while it lasted.

On another project, the team wasn't given cubicles for the first few months. We were all jammed in small, unventilated team rooms, where you always knew what everyone had for lunch and who went to the gym instead. In a desperate effort to limit the variety of smells in the room, one team member started handing out chewing gum after lunch every day.

On this particular afternoon, the constant chomping and smacking noises were too much for one man and he blew his top. "For gosh sakes, please!!! You sound like...I don't even know what...something disgusting, that's for sure. Are you trying to kill the gum? Or me? Can you please, please, please shut your mouth when you chew? Man! I can't stand it!"

He wasn't wrong. The chewing did sound (and look) pretty gross, but he handled it wrong. He let it get to him and then he spoke without thinking. Furthermore, he didn't check around for allies before going on the attack. For weeks afterward, he couldn't walk into a room without four or five people smacking their gum at him and laughing.

If you are a consultant, it's often easier for your teammates to get you fired (or re-assigned) than to learn to live with your annoying habits.

If you are a consultant, it's often easier for your teammates to get you fired (or re-assigned) than to learn to live with your annoying habits. Job security is all about getting along and fitting in, so you do not want to be the most annoying guy on the project team!

It's also about recognizing that you probably are that guy sometimes and being a little bit more patient with your colleagues as a result.

That Guy In A Meeting

Don't be any of these guys, either.

Pontification Man – This guy goes on and on, telling you what he's going to say, saying it, and then telling you what he said.

Um Man – To avoid losing control of the conversation, this guy fills every pause with "Um," not realizing that he might be able to think better if he weren't talking

Too Much Detail Man – 'nuff said

50,000 Foot-Only Man – He is eloquent when you talk about the big picture, but refuses to allow anyone to get into the details...which we all know is where the real work gets done. Unless you're the CEO of a multi-national corporation, you have to be willing to work at any altitude.

Hypnotized-by-Email Man – If you go to the trouble to think of a meeting topic, send out an invitation, invent an agenda and prepare slides, you naturally expect the people who show up for your meeting to pay attention while you talk. Wireless technology has made it possible for people to multi-task very effectively, but there is nothing more defeating than presenting to the tops of people's heads because everyone at the conference table is hunched over his laptop.

Buzzword Man – This guy is annoying in meetings, in team rooms and in cubicles. In fact, this guy is just plain annoying all the time.

Foul Language Man – Much like Buzzword Man, this guy is obviously too lazy to think of the right words to express what he thinking, if indeed he is thinking at all, but this guy isn't trying to impress you with his knowledge. He isn't trying to impress you at all. He doesn't care what you think of him.

Reiteration Man – If the only contribution you have to make in a meeting is to restate what has already been said, you don't have any contribution to make.

Too-Busy-To-Be-Prompt Man – If you are always late to every meeting, there is something wrong with the way you manage your schedule or your time. Fix this behavior. It's rude.

Can't-Control-the-Meeting Man and his arch-nemesis, Wants-To-Take-Over-the-Meeting Man

Secondary-Conversation People – These folks are only annoying if their conversation is less interesting than the meeting.

Disagrees-With-Everything Man – This guy honestly believes he is just being practical, or serving as the Voice of Reason, or playing Devil's Advocate. This may be true sometimes, and even helpful occasionally, but when it becomes a habit, everyone else just tunes him out. Don't give up your influence by being this guy.

Obscure Metaphor Man – This guy is as annoying as the fool in a troupe of Morris dancers. (See? Wasn't that annoying?)

That Guy In a Team Room

Project teams often work together in a team room, rather than in individual cubicles or offices. Sharing workspace creates its own unique opportunities for annoying work habits.

Gum-Smacker – Some people can chew gum and no one even knows they are doing it. If you aren't one of these people, be prepared for complaints. It's surprising how many people list this as their only pet peeve.

Bloviating Man – This guy can't stop talking. The dictionary defines bloviate as "to speak pompously and excessively".

Too-Much-Information Man – He tells long stories about his personal life, in excruciating and embarrassing detail, distracting everyone from work and preventing others from telling interesting stories.

Intrusive-Personal-Life Man – His wife calls three or four times every day, and he always takes the call because there is always a crisis at home. His mother has shingles and his dog chewed up the power cord for his company-issue laptop.

B.O. Man and his wife, Too-Much-Perfume Lady

Instant Best Friend – Joining a new project team or workgroup, particularly in a new company where you don't know anyone, is often intimidating. People are more likely to help you if you are generally self-sufficient. Don't be afraid to ask for help, but don't become so clingy that you annoy people.

Constant Cougher – There's illness and then there's the nervous cough. If it's illness, go home. Germs spread faster in a team room than in a daycare center. If it's a nervous habit, you are probably annoying people.

Constant-Humming Man – You either think this guy doesn't exist or you've seriously considered killing him.

Smokey the Bear – This guy is never around because he's always standing outside the building surrounded by other smokers. If you think you're annoyed, just imagine how the guy who pays his bill feels.

Communication Moves

Once you understand the Fundamental Moves, it's time to really flex those consulting muscles: the ears, the brain and the tongue. In that order.

Many large consulting firms recruit recent college graduates and place them directly into large projects with the expectation that they will learn consulting skills from colleagues and on-the-job training. This is a proven and effective way to learn consulting and we know many successful consultants who started out with no previous business experience.

For them, learning the basic Communication Moves was the highest priority. Every other lesson depended on their willingness to ask questions and ability to listen.

Consulting engagements typically start with gathering information and then move on to distributing information, so we address these issues in the same order here.

The Communication Moves are:

- *Listen* intently to everything.

- *Ask* good questions and then listen again.

- Create word pictures to communicate your message. *A metaphor is worth ten-thousand words*.

- Prepare diligently for *presentations*.

- *Use the right format to deliver information*.

- Manage *meetings* efficiently and effectively.

- Learn how to conduct *System Training* so that your students learn what they really need to know to do their jobs.

In addition to getting along with people, communicating with people is an important part of the consultant's role.

"Someday there will be a telephone in every major city in America."

Alexander Graham Bell

Listen

You might not know this, but it is frustrating to talk to someone while their eyes dart around the room as they look for someone more interesting to talk to. People can tell when you are not listening and are instead thinking of what you are going to say when they finally finish.

For consultants, listening is an absolutely critical skill.

Listen to your clients. Especially the ones closest to the action. When the assembly line foreman is explaining why his team can't scan the barcode serial numbers on each part as they go down the conveyor belt, you do not want to be the consultant who ignores what may be perceived as "whining" and fails to document the issue. Later, when your project goes live and manufacturing grinds to a halt while the people on the shop floor struggle to fit all the new steps into their routine, you will be at fault for ignoring the issue.

Listen to your clients. Especially the ones closest to the action.

If you had listened to the foreman during the early discussion, instead of dismissing him altogether, you might have been able to resolve the issue with a change to the process or at least made sure that everyone at every level of corporate leadership was aware and had pre-approved the disaster.

As outsiders, consultants often have an advantage in problem solving. The people who are closest to the issue may not be able to see simple flaws in their business processes. Therefore, careful listening will afford you the opportunity to add value for your customer even when the topic of conversation is not directly related to your role. After your client has described the issue, it is your job to apply critical thinking and problem-solving skills to resolve it. Don't forget that it is the client's job to get back to work running their broken process. Their brokenness is the reason you have a job. Embrace it for what it is: an opportunity to help your client.

We know one consultant who has taken the art of patient listening to a level that often seems superhuman. When you talk with him, you know that you have his undivided attention. No matter how long, tedious or repetitive your conversation may be, he will listen with eager, focused attention. He only interrupts with appropriate questions and never seems distracted or bored by the subject matter. And he'd be the first to tell you that he has unearthed and solved issues with this technique more than any other in his consulting toolbox. It's unnerving to watch, but highly flattering when you are part of the conversation.

Multi-Lingual Listening

Whether or not English is your first language, you are likely to find yourself working closely with people whose first language is different than yours on project teams. This is especially true on IT projects, which often include team members from all over the globe.

Proactive, careful listening is important in every relationship, but in communication where one or both speakers are using a second language, it is essential.

The temptation to give up half way through the conversation, to assume the other person knows what you were saying, or to find someone else who is easier to talk to...these are big risk factors in trying to get things done. Develop the relationships on other topics. In other words, recognize that you are going to need good relationships with everyone on the team, even those you find hard to talk to. Work hard in advance with them, so you don't have to try to build a relationship while you are negotiating a tricky compromise or trying to resolve a problem together.

Tips:

Listen carefully. Restate what you have heard. Repetition is less frustrating to people who are trying to communicate in a second (or third) language.

Remember that tone of voice, emotions like impatience and frustration, and rudeness are universally understood. You must suppress yours and sympathize with theirs. Be the more generous communicator.

It's absolutely never okay to mock or make fun of someone else's accent or vocabulary. Unless, of course, they make fun of yours first (just kidding...never means *never*.) Also, never assume you know where someone comes from. It's easy, unless you are very well-traveled, to mistake an accent or name as being from one place of origin when it's really somewhere else entirely. Once, when traveling to Chicago, a consultant mistakenly assumed his cab driver was of one nationality when, in reality, the driver was from a rival nation. He spent the whole cab ride listening to frightening inter-cultural bashing and learned a valuable lesson to apply at client sites.

On the other hand, it is perfectly okay to ask sincere questions about their culture, language or impressions. In fact, we often go to our colleagues who learned English as a second language with grammar questions and for help in communicating with others who are less fluent in English. Handled correctly, this is a compliment to their education and teamwork. Handled incorrectly, it can be condescending or make them feel like outsiders when they've gone to all the trouble to learn English in order to be insiders. Be conscious, not paranoid.

You Don't Know What You Don't Know

Many years ago, we were hired by a client to provide training in team-building and productivity tools for several offices in the United States and in Europe. The participants in the U.S. classes went through the material without a hitch, but we encountered problem after problem with the offices in France and Belgium. Even though the training was mandated by their headquarters and the schedule of available classes was flexible enough to make it easy for any employee in the department to attend, only a small fraction of the employees signed up.

We eventually sat down with several managers in the Antwerp office to try to find out what the problem was. No one on our team spoke French and the Antwerp team's English was limited, plus there was a thirty year age difference between our team and most of the employees in the European offices.

The managers were distrustful of us from the first moment. They were defensive and hostile, stubbornly repeating their employees' excuses for avoiding the training and allowing no room for negotiation in the discussion. We were equally stubborn, continuing to repeat various bits from our sales pitch in a futile effort to convince the managers that there was value in these classes. Both sides were talking and no one was listening.

Finally the breakthrough came just when it appeared that our trip had been wasted and these people would never agree to the training. One of the Belgian managers, an older man, turned to a member of our team and said, "How old are you?"

Our guy answered, "Twenty-six, sir."

"What year were you born?"

"1964."

The man turned to his colleagues and began speaking rapid French. They answered with laughter and more French. We sat in confused silence while they talked for a few minutes and then the man turned back to us and said, in a much friendlier tone, "We now understand. You are not rude or disrespectful. You are stupid."

Another manager at the table saw our expressions and rushed to correct him. "No, Maurice. They are not stupid. They are ignorant. Different meaning." He turned to us. "You do not know what happened here during the Nazi Occupation in the 1940's."

He went on to explain that both French and Belgian citizens who were friendly to the Nazi soldiers during the war were considered traitors by their countrymen. Their activities were described as "collaborating with the enemy" and the word Collaborator is still considered a grave insult in those countries.

Our course was titled "Tools and Techniques for Collaboration" and their employees' emotional reaction to the title and description was an impassable roadblock. Although they weren't consciously aware of it, the managers and employees were treating us as enemies, so much so that they had not even been willing to tell us what their real objection was and instead instinctively manufactured other excuses.

We changed the name of the course and learned a valuable lesson about listening instead of talking when trying to resolve problems.

Ask

When we start working with a new client or department, our first priority is usually to learn how that company works. We walk around. We talk to people. We ask a lot of questions. One of our favorites is "Why?"

Back in the 90's, we worked with a client who was implementing an ERP system to run their manufacturing, shipping and financial systems. While we were preparing the training materials, toward the end of the project, we did a complete inventory of every employee's responsibilities to help identify who would need training in which tasks. This is how we found Fred.

It's always better to ask than to guess, assume or wonder.

Fred's whole job was to file the "FedEx pinks". If you were working in any office in America at that time, you know that the "pink" was the third sheet in the Federal Express address/ticket form. When the driver picked up your package, he left the "pink" behind.

At this small company, Federal Express, UPS and other couriers were commonly used by nearly every employee. Hundreds of packages travelled in or out of the various corporate locations every week. Fred's job was to file these pinks and later, when the bills arrived, to match the pinks to a copy of the paid invoice and then re-file them. Naturally we asked, "Why?"

We had assumed that Fred would later analyze the shipping patterns in these records, or use the information to negotiate volume discounts with the carriers, or something. Fred didn't know why the pinks were matched and stored. He just did his job every day. We kept asking why until we traced the policy back to a former employee who had been caught sending a personal package on the corporate FedEx account. To prevent this kind of embezzlement in the future, management instituted a policy to match all pinks (sent by approved employees for authorized shipments) against the invoice to be sure that no charges appeared on the invoice that were not legitimate company business.

As the company grew, the job of managing the pinks grew until it became a whole job in itself. Fred's job. When we really looked at the numbers, we found that if every employee sent four unauthorized overnight packages a year, it would still be cheaper to just pay the cost than to track and catch them.

Fred was reassigned to Security, which he liked much better, and the stored pinks were destroyed. We also recommended the development of an automated tracking and analysis tool for courier shipments, since just letting your employees steal from you didn't seem like a great idea either.

Ask lots of questions. You have to ask questions to discover expectations, to learn rules and protocol, to understand business processes, to build relationships, and to get feedback. It's always better to ask than to guess, assume or wonder.

Working with IT systems and projects, much of our work has revolved around business requirements. Every IT project starts with an objective or purpose, and then someone collects all the business requirements that must be met by whatever solution is devised. Until the business requirements are nailed down and signed off, you can rightly claim that you can't produce a reliable solution.

One of the most common requirements is, "I need this report," accompanied by a thick printout with many columns of numbers. We sometimes find a nicer way to say, but our response is always the same, "Why?" We never accept a blanket requirement like that without digging deeper. What do you use the report for?

How often do you run the report? Which data, specifically, are you seeking when you run it?

Often, we find that the report is considered a requirement for the new system simply because it is printed and distributed today. Further investigation may reveal that a single field or column of data is actually used for analysis, and that data may be more easily obtained from another source.

Keep asking questions until you not only understand what is required, but also why it is required.

You can even ask the dumb questions, but carefully consider who you will ask. You've heard time and again that there are no dumb questions, but you also know that it's not entirely true. There are questions that it would be dumb to ask your client, but that you can ask your team lead or project manager. There are questions for which you think you should already know the answer, so you don't ask for fear of looking dumb. Take a moment to consider who to ask, and then ask the questions that might make you look dumb anyway. Not asking is worse.

Questions to ask the customer:

- Do you mind if I keep my laptop open and take notes while we talk?

- Do you prefer donuts or breakfast tacos for our morning meetings?

Questions to ask the Project Manager when the customer is not around:

- How much pressure should we put on the client to meet these deadlines?

- I'm going to lunch with one of the users. Should I pay for his lunch, too?

The exception questions that really are too dumb to ask anyone because you should already know the answers:

- Is it okay to charge adult movies to my hotel room and put them on my expense report?

- Is your secretary single?

- Why are you going to the doctor?

- Have you ever heard of a business opportunity called Amway?

A well-crafted, well-timed question can actually make you look smart and engaged and even brave. Project teams occasionally develop elephants in the room, which are big smelly problems that exist outside the specific day-to-day tasks but affect progress and are a potential risk to success. Asking questions about these challenges when no one else is willing to acknowledge them is brave, but this must be handled carefully.

Awkward Questions

We were once in this situation at Biggish Inc. Our project, which was relatively small and insignificant, was on a path that would take us into direct conflict with a much larger, high profile project that was stuck in an analysis whirlpool. In a team meeting with representatives from our project team and Biggish management, we asked the question, "Given the...<grinning broadly>...uh... inertia...that exists on the [other] project, how can we as a team approach our project's next phase, *and* engage the other project team, and still hope to make progress?"

The project manager (a consultant) turned white, but the Biggish senior manager in the room laughed and said, "That's a very good way to ask that question. Very diplomatic." (When this happens, do not beam with pride. Nod as if you hear it all the time.) He went on to explain his plan for circumventing the obstacles presented by the other project and everyone left the meeting feeling more optimistic and better prepared.

This was the best possible outcome. We looked smart and were not called on to either defend our observation or present a solution. But there are several other things that could have happened.

Management could have pretended they had no knowledge of the problem, gotten defensive, and asked us to prove it existed. If we had appeared to be criticizing the other project team, we could have been labeled opportunistic trouble-makers.

Alternatively, the manager who laughed could have turned it around on us and said, "I'm not sure. What do you recommend? What would you do?" If this happens, you should already be in *consulting stance* and your answer should be ready. Remember that you've asked the question and the customer has said he doesn't know, so this is not a good time to act like it is an easy question. In fact, it's perfectly acceptable to say, "I don't know. Let me give it some thought and let's talk about it tomorrow."

If you believe you know exactly what should be done to resolve the elephant problem, present your solution as a question, too. At this meeting, we might have said, "What would happen if we sat down with the other project's PM and tried to reconcile the conflicts in the project plan?" Or possibly, "Is there any way to involve the [Director, Program Manager, VP, CIO] who ultimately owns both projects, to try to find a solution?" In the beginning of a client relationship, it is wise to trust your customer's instincts about navigating corporate politics. In the long run, it's their career on the line, not yours. However, they may prove to be inept or oblivious about corporate politics, in which case you should tread carefully and perhaps ask around for advice.

Almost any good idea can be presented as a question. If it's really the right answer, everyone in the room will think they came up with the solution, but they'll remember that you were the one who first asked the question.

Hidden Agendas

Look for the real, underlying question, issue or need. If you understand what motivates people, it'll be easier to persuade them to your view.

Look for the real, underlying question, issue or need.

When you see the words "hidden agenda", you may think of ulterior motives or secret conspiracies, and no doubt those may exist. But we are also talking about priorities that are not obvious to you, motives that have not yet been identified and secondary considerations that may be affecting another person's decision-making. In order to be effective, you have to discover what these are.

Six Sigma uses the "Five Whys" to determine the root cause of a problem. For example, to diagnose a car problem, you might ask five whys.

Problem: The "Service Engine Soon" light on my dashboard is lit.

1. Why? Because the engine is not idling smoothly.

2. Why? Because the idle regulator is malfunctioning.

3. Why? Because the valve is sticking.

4. Why? Because there is sticky residue in the mechanism.

5. Why? Because it has not been cleaned in five years.

This is a simple example, but it's a simple process. For technical issues, most engineers and developers rely on some form of this method to solve every problem. It's commonly referred to as deductive reasoning, and it can make you terribly effective at rooting out core issues.

In a relational context, the Five Whys is even more valuable. People also often have complex root causes involving multiple mechanisms under a variety of influences. To understand why someone disagrees with you or is reluctant to make a decision, you can usually just ask "why?" several times.

Mr. Smith: Upgrading the accounting system is not an option.

Bob: **Why**?

Mr. Smith: It's too expensive.

Bob: **Why** do you think it will be expensive? The vendor said they'll give us the newer software for free just to get us off the old version.

Mr. Smith: It will take a long time and we can't afford to pay your consulting fees for that long.

Bob: **Why** will it take so long?

Mr. Smith: Because all the interfaces will have to be re-written.

Bob: **Why** will the interfaces have to be re-written?

Mr. Smith: Because you said the newer version has data validation and our satellite systems are full of bad data.

Bob: **Why** do we want to keep putting bad data into the accounting system?

Mr. Smith: Because that's how we do it now. Who knows what the impact on our financial reports would be if we started getting accurate data? Now go away and leave me alone!

With only five whys, Bob was able to discover exactly what was standing in the way of the upgrade his client's system needed. Bob saved himself a great deal of frustration and ultimately turned this to his advantage. He sold his client a finance consulting project in which the current financial reports were validated, much of the bad data in the satellite systems was cleaned up, and eventually, the old accounting system was finally upgraded.

Throughout the process, the relationship between Bob's consulting firm and Mr. Smith's company was protected and strengthened because Bob understood the underlying motives behind his client's decisions.

Ask questions to uncover the secondary priorities and you will be successful.

Execution Tip: There is only one right way to do the Five Whys and dozens of wrong ways. Your facial expressions and tone of voice cannot show a trace of suspicion, judgment or frustration. Your questions have to come from a genuine curiosity and your attitude has to be sympathetic throughout. Otherwise, when Mr. Smith says "Go away and leave me alone!", he might really mean it.

The Paradox

It's counter-intuitive, but the best way to make someone think you are smart is to ask questions. In conversation, if a customer mentions a business term or acronym that you don't know, ask for more information. This makes them feel smart and shows that you have enough confidence in your knowledge to expose your ignorance. Plus, you get to learn something new and will look even smarter to the next person.

A Metaphor is Worth Ten-Thousand Words

A powerful word picture will do the heavy lifting in a conversation the same way a jack lifts your car so you can change the tire. Work hard to find the right word picture for the message you want to communicate.

"How's your project going?"
"Down in flames."

That's pretty vivid, but is it accurate? Is it productive? Probably not. The next one is both funny and positive, but obviously refers to a totally different project. We hope.

"You're going live next week, right? So this project is nearly over?"
"The fat lady is getting her hair done and warming up her vocal cords."

As consultants, we often find ourselves trying to persuade people to see things the way we see them or to enlist others to support our proposal. This can be something small, like increasing the number of daily uploads from one to two, or something huge, like combining three separate instances into one global system. In either case, the argument that "the consultant recommends it" might not be sufficient.

A good word picture won't replace a good idea, but it will help you communicate your idea to someone else.

If you want people to get behind your proposal, you need to get them emotionally invested. If you want them to then advocate your proposal to others, you need to give them a message that is easy to remember and repeat.

When we talk to leaders in consulting firms about the value of training their teams in consulting skills, we don't use slide decks full of bullet point and statistics. There is nothing we can tell them about their challenges that they don't already know.

Instead, we start like this...

What if a pro football coach ran his team the way we run our teams in the consulting industry? What if he said to himself, "These guys have a lot of experience. They won a lot of games last year. We'll skip training and I'll just tell them to come in for the first game, suit up, and we'll figure it out as we go along."

How would that first game go? Would they win?

This short word picture, which creates a vivid and humorous image in the leader's mind, replaces a multitude of bullet points. It is memorable enough for them to repeat later to others, so the key message from our meeting is more likely to be circulated among their leadership team.

A good word picture won't replace a good idea, but it will help you communicate your idea to someone else.

The metaphor doesn't have to be perfect, but you should also be prepared for the laughing objections. Our prospects might say, "But football teams have to practice. Their opponents play by specific rules with a specific level of training," to which we say, "Okay, picture the same game on Sunday if both teams blow off training. Is it better? I mean, I would pay a lot of money to see that game, but is it football?"

Or they might say, "Yeah, but on our projects, there isn't another team trying to stop us from scoring," to which we say, "Okay, then make it the marching band. What if they skipped training?" You don't have to convince them that it's exactly the same. Your goal is to make an analogy that they can take away from the meeting and discuss with others.

We were frustrated for a while with one IT Manager at Biggish who treated everyone who had technical skills as if they were interchangeable.   He would assign tasks based entirely on availability with no regard for the individual's skills or unique experience. The argument that finally got his attention was, "Mr. Smith, you are missing a great strategic advantage. It's like you are playing checkers with a chess set."

In politics, they call this the 10-Word Answer. If you can create an image, state your position, include all your arguments, and draw an emotional response from your audience (laughter is an emotional response) in ten words, then you have found a powerful communication tool.   "It's like you are playing checkers with a chess set" does all of this.

It's an advantage, usually, for your word picture to be funny enough to be repeated, especially if you want everyone to get the message. Be prepared for only part of your message to get out, though. While training the users on a new Purchasing system, we heard one instructor say that the users would be "as happy as squirrels in a nut factory" when the project went live. Later, it was all over Biggish that the instructor called their company a nut factory.

Presentations

Formal presentations are a common occurrence in a consultant's life and being able to present effectively is a basic move in your Consulting Stance skill set.

If you are afraid to stand up and speak in front of people, and studies have shown that people fear this more than death or the IRS, there are things you can do to improve your confidence and eliminate the worst of the fear. Everyone feels a little anxiety before they make a presentation, but if you can get rid of the visible sweat on your upper lip and that nervous twitch in your left shoulder, your audience will be able to concentrate on the information you are providing.

The keys to effective presentation skills are *practice* and *feedback*.

> *The keys to effective presentation skills are practice and feedback.*

Volunteer to conduct as many presentations as you can. If you are working on a small team, be the one who offers to speak when the project manager comes in and asks for an update on your status. Later, ask both the project manager and someone else in the room for feedback. Ask them separately and privately, so that you can be sure you are getting honest information.

Join Toastmasters, if there is a chapter available to you. This is a great place to learn to speak in public and to get practice in a supportive environment where productive feedback is readily available.

With important presentations, practice what you are going to say in advance. Extemporaneous speaking is never as well-organized or smoothly executed as a planned speech. If they're available, enlist supportive colleagues to listen and give you feedback; otherwise, enlist your family, friends or other people you trust to provide honest and helpful feedback.

Know Your Audience

Biggish engaged us to develop a comprehensive global strategy for one segment of the IT infrastructure. We spent weeks investigating requirements, researching alternatives, devising a strategy and developing a detailed approach for how to reach our objectives over the next ten years. The program was ambitious and included many different facets.

In the course of this larger effort, we identified a weakness in one aspect of the IT operation and determined that a complete overhaul of project governance in IT was needed, regardless of whether our overall strategy was adopted. Rather than fold our recommendations for project governance into our findings and recommendations at the end of our project, we decided to produce a separate recommendation that could be adopted immediately.

Once we had a solution, we began to prepare our presentation. We divided our audience into two general groups: managers who knew there was a problem and those who did not. We added the managers that we had not talked with during our research to the group that did not know there was a problem.

When we presented our findings, we spent very little time defining the problem with the audience who already knew it existed, and instead jumped directly into the details of our solution. This audience would have been impatient with a presentation that included too much information they already knew. They would have felt we were wasting their time, which is never a good idea.

With the second group, we started by discussing our investigation and the issues we discovered before leading them to the conclusion that a problem existed, and only then presented our solution to the problem. For this audience, time spent discussing the solution would have felt like a waste of time if it happened before they recognized the problem. Why fix something that isn't broken?

When You Practice, Check the Time

Ideally, your material should take no more than 20 minutes to present. While employees in Corporate America have developed a high tolerance for meetings, they are typically only willing to give up an hour out of their calendar for any one meeting. With getting-settled and packing-up-to-leave time taken off the beginning and end of the hour, your actual meeting time is usually about 40 minutes. If you allow time for interruptions and questions, you are left with approximately 20 minutes of actual presentation time.

With proper planning and practice, you look poised and professional during your presentation.

As a general rule of thumb, a typical slide in a presentation takes a minimum of three minutes to present. Plan accordingly.

With proper planning and practice, you look poised and professional during your presentation. Without it, you may have to rush through the second half of your material or allow the meeting to run over the scheduled time. Neither enhances your professional image.

Organizing Your Presentation

One of the most common presentation situations for a consultant is when you are asked to present your team's recommendation for resolving a particular issue. Once again, how you organize the presentation depends as much on your audience as it does on the material you are presenting.

If you want to show the value you provide and you have a somewhat captive audience, you may choose to organize your presentation as a chronological narrative that summarizes your activities, such as:

I.   The Issue, as you originally understood it

II.   Your Investigation, including the number of people interviewed and a sample or summary of your findings

III.   Alternatives Considered, including a summary of the pros and cons identified

IV.   Preliminary Solution, including reasons for selection

V.   Testing conducted to validate the solution

VI.   Your Recommendation

VII.   Proposed Approach

With this organization, you include the details of your findings in each section of the presentation and you have the opportunity to gauge your audience's level of acceptance at each step along the way. For example, you wouldn't move on to describe how you tested your solution until you were sure your audience understood how you selected it from the alternatives.

Presenting the same information to upper management, who are notoriously impatient with narrative presentations, might require a totally different and much shorter agenda, particularly if they are the ones who originally told you the problem existed. In that case, you might organize your presentation this way:

I.   Summary of Issue

II.   Your Recommendation

III.   Proposed Approach

IV.   Supporting Evidence

      a.   Details of investigation and research

      b.   Alternatives considered, including pros and cons of each

      c.   Selection criteria for solution

      d.   Testing and validation activities

It's important to have all the same supporting documentation available to you because you want to be prepared to answer any questions that may arise.

In either case, it is important to begin the presentation with an overview of how you intend to present the information. People are more tolerant if they understand your agenda, whether you are leading them through the suspenseful narrative or presenting a conclusion and waiting for them to ask questions to find out how you reached it.

Questions and Objections

When you are presenting material that you prepared, every question or objection may seem like an attack. (You are standing alone in front of a conference room full of people who are firing questions at you...of course it feels like an attack!) If you get defensive or show any resentment at the questions, your audience will see weakness and ego. They will think you are weak because your argument doesn't seem to stand up to reasonable discussion, which is what their questions seem like from their side. They may think you are arrogant because you are unwilling to have your conclusions challenged.

Instead, listen carefully to each question, objection or suggestion and respond as though the attacker is being helpful.

"What's wrong with [rejected alternative]? Wouldn't that be cheaper?"

"Thank you for bringing that up. Yes, [rejected alternative] would be cheaper and we seriously considered it. However, we discovered that it would only solve half the problem and that it would really only buy us some time before we had to go with [selected alternative] anyway. At that point, you might feel that we had wasted time and money with the first solution."

When someone challenges your base assumptions, as opposed to your conclusions, concede most of their point, if you possibly can, before restating your perspective.

"I think you are overstating the issue. Things work fine most of the time. Why should we change anything?"

"That's a good point. We focused our attention on the times when a problem occurred and looked for a way to prevent those problems, You're absolutely right that these problems are rare, but they can be very expensive. For instance,..."

Managing Participation

If you are doing a presentation, particularly if you are using a slide deck, stand up. This establishes your authority in the meeting and encourages people to pay attention to you.

This works even if you are in a small team room. If you want to limit discussion and keep attention focused on you, get out of your chair and stand by the whiteboard with a pen in your hand. Even if you don't write anything, and you probably will, this gives you a reason to be standing. When you are standing, you are in charge.

If you want to encourage participation and open discussion, the reverse applies. Sit down. The people in the room may not know why they feel free to talk now, but they will.

When you are ready to end the conversation, stand up. The person who is talking when you stand up will finish his thought, but when he stops talking, you'll see all eyes back on you.

Open With a Joke

The conventional wisdom for speeches and presentations is that you should begin with a joke or humorous observation to establish a bond with the audience. For some speakers, this is an effective tool that helps them relax. For others, it feels (and looks) fake. You already know which category you fall into. If it helps you, do it. If not, don't force it.

If you do a lot of presentations or training classes, you'll soon develop a collection of anecdotes and stories that illustrate the points you make often.

When you tell jokes or stories, always consider who your audience is.

One consultant who often taught classes in her particular application specialty had a fairly noticeable southern accent. As part of her training, she got into the habit of telling stories from her childhood that poked fun at her Texas roots and entertained the class while they waited, for instance, for a query to run on their systems. Over time, the stories evolved from pure fact to a more humorous interpretation of fact to, eventually, outright fiction.

This was not a problem and would never have mattered, except that she was assigned to teach these training classes at the company where her mother worked as a senior executive. Imagine Mom's surprise, sitting in a board meeting, when she learned that her daughter was ten before she discovered that her Uncle Bob didn't invent "bob-wire" (barbed wire). The bigger surprise, of course, was the discovery that her daughter had an Uncle Bob.

When you tell stories, always consider your audience.

Use the Right Format to Deliver Information

The quality of your communication defines the quality of your work. Every presentation, document, report and email message contributes to the impression your customers have of your abilities and professionalism.

With each communication, consider what impression you want to leave with the reader. We've worked with gifted system architects and engineers who did not take time to effectively communicate their ideas, and therefore did not receive the respect they deserved. We've also worked with many consultants with average technical skills or limited business experience who more than compensated with the quality of their documentation.

At many corporations, a slide deck is mandatory for every meeting. Many professionals use slides to communicate every possible message, without considering whether this is the best way to convey the specific information in question.

We've worked on teams where the first step in preparing a deliverable was to create a series of blank slides with titles and then to gather the information needed to fill in each slide. If you've been working this way for a long time, it probably feels natural to you, so you assume it is the best way. It's not.

Instead, gather the information you want to present first. Then, lay it out in front of you where you can see it. This might require printing a series of reports, writing notes on index cards or just making a list on a whiteboard. Once you can really see everything you have collected or created, you can judge what actually belongs in your document or presentation.

It's extremely unlikely that everything needs to go into the slide deck you will use for a meeting. Answer these questions first:

- What is the purpose of this communication?

- What is my one key point?

- What do I want the reader to do with this information?

Ask yourself if it might be more effective to prepare a short slide presentation and hand out a thicker narrative report that contains all the details and can be forwarded to others as a standalone communication.

A presentation is never just about the facts. Slides should provide emotional proof that what you are saying is true. Show, rather than tell.

This is a great example of a cluttered slide that actually has a simple message. The whole thing can be summarized as "We're cheaper," but that wouldn't be as powerful.

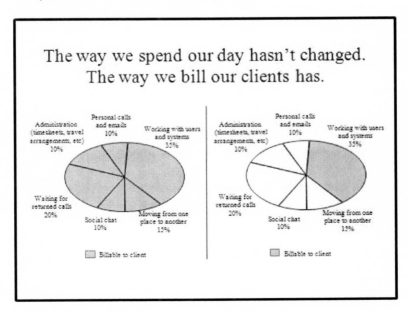

Most of the slides we use in our workshops are very simple. We want the audience to be listening to us, not reading bullet points.

There are times when only a busy slide will convey the message you want the audience to get. Here's another example of a cluttered slide with a simple message. This example was created to explain the user's path through a commercial training website.

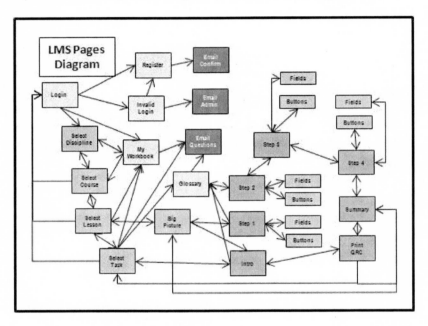

It looks like a spider web, doesn't it? The message the speaker wanted to convey with this slide was that the system in question is extremely complex and testing will require time and resources to complete. That message comes through loud and clear.

If, instead, the speaker had intended for the audience to get a clear understanding of the purpose and effect of each page from this slide, it's too crowded and complicated.

Use graphics to simplify or amplify your message. We've included several good books on this subject in the chapter at the back of this book called "Recommended Reading".

Meetings

Sometimes it feels like a consultant's primary role is to schedule meetings, conduct meetings and sit in meetings. Meetings are where information is exchanged and decisions are made. Meetings are the lifeblood of projects and consulting engagements and they are often the only time your customer will see you.

Meeting Ground Rules

We include the following list of Meeting Ground Rules in every meeting invitation we send out, regardless of audience or topic, just below the Agenda. After they receive it two or three times, our invitees know that the rules aren't directed at them personally, but they also know that we are serious about enforcing them in every meeting.

Our project team is committed to efficient meetings. We promise not to waste your time. In return, we ask the following of all meeting attendees:

- *Please arrive on time.*

- *Please silence cell phones.*

- *Please close laptops.*

- *Please limit discussion of items not listed on today's agenda.*

- *Please participate in the meeting discussion. You are invited to this meeting because your input is necessary to the successful completion of this project.*

If you have any questions about these guidelines, please feel free to contact me before the meeting.

We rarely have to enforce the ground rules ourselves. Because they were published to the entire meeting in advance, attendees enforce the rules with each other, allowing us to focus on the meeting itself.

Agendas and Notes

It's okay to have a meeting without slides. It's not okay to have a meeting without a purpose or an agenda (even if there is only one item on the agenda). If you are scheduling the meeting, include the agenda in the meeting invitation when you send it out. This will help people determine whether or not they should attend your meeting.

Often, your agenda will prompt invitees to bring other people with them, making the meeting much more effective. Furthermore, having to think through your agenda, and remembering the "27 Moves" chapter, you will be able to predict potential responses to the agenda and how the meeting might go.

It's okay to have a meeting without slides. It's not okay to have a meeting without a purpose or an agenda.

Following this rule will make your meetings incredibly effective, which will make it easier to get people to attend them.

After the meeting, the organizer or scribe should distribute meeting notes. There may be days or weeks where this is the only tangible evidence of your presence, so don't underestimate the value of volunteering to be the scribe in a meeting.

If you are tasked with taking notes, it's not important to capture every point made by every participant. Instead, consider what meeting notes are really used for, and capture the following:

- Topics discussed, including a summary of the discussion for each topic

- Action items, including who took ownership for the action and when they are due

- Decisions made, and the reasons for the decisions, if appropriate

Meeting notes provide documentation for task assignments and decisions, and are often circulated to provide information to people who did not attend the meeting.

Avoid Distractions

Set the expectation early that background and secondary conversations are not going to be tolerated. Unfortunately, this is the one rule that is nearly impossible to enforce unless you are constantly alert for infractions. When a secondary conversation starts, even if it's not loud enough to intrude on the meeting, stop the meeting and listen until it's finished. Staring at the offenders and listening to their conversation will usually stop the behavior quickly.

If you allow one background conversation, others will start. If the whole group is listening, most people will stop talking, unless their conversation is relevant to the meeting. Some people will continue their conversation anyway, but hopefully you have prevented others from starting.

If people stop paying attention, use their names to get them back. We were in a meeting recently and started exchanging notes about this chapter...so we quickly lost interest in the meeting itself. The facilitator noticed and deftly recalled our attention by saying, "We're moving into the AR area now, so Christine will be answering the hard questions and Casey can stand down." Neither of us was actually being called on, but we both looked up and started paying attention.

Off-Topic Discussions

When you are running a large meeting with a long agenda, you must keep the meeting on topic and moving forward. One of the most frustrating complications you can face is "rat-hole discussions" involving people who outrank you.

An effective way to deal with these distractions is to write "Parking Lot" at the top of a section of whiteboard or on an easel pad and explain at the beginning of the meeting that this is where you will document new topics that come up during the meeting.

When the discussion veers off your agenda, say, "This seems to be a very important point that needs clarification. Let's get it on the list and schedule a separate meeting for it." This will acknowledge the importance of the issue and may shut down the immediate conversation. If not, tap into your reserve of patience and just let the discussion go on for a while. If you aren't involved in the rat-hole conversation, use this opportunity to review the rest of the agenda and determine where the lost time can be made up.

Productive Conflict

Don't be afraid of animated discussion in meetings. Conflict is healthy and necessary to be sure that all ideas are heard and all opinions receive appropriate consideration.

Since consultants are often the outsiders in confrontational meetings, your role may become that of the referee. When a conflict starts, your role is to be sure that everyone gets to speak. You might have to say, "Hold on. Try not to interrupt each other. Everyone should get a chance to be heard," or "We haven't heard from you, Ted. What do you think?"

If the conflict escalates into personal attacks or strays off the topic, the referee analogy gives you the two tools you'll need. If someone says something personal, you can call "Foul!" If the conversation goes into other topics or people begin to repeat themselves, make a "T" with your hands and call a "Time out!" This allows you to take control of the meeting.

Don't forget to thank the participants after an animated debate. If they cared about the issue enough to join the discussion, they are valuable to your project.

System Training

Consultants are often called upon to teach the new system, either to key users in preparation for testing, or to the entire user community. Whether you are teaching a week-long class on how to use a new software application or doing desk-side training with one user, there are some important things to remember.

Enthusiasm for the subject and a positive attitude toward the project are the most important things the instructor can bring to any applications training session. Students take their cue from the instructor and they will learn much faster if they start with an optimistic attitude.

You Cannot Move Too Slowly

A carefully controlled pace is the second most important thing you will need. Slow down, particularly through the early lessons. You know your material, so it seems very simple to you. Slow down anyway. You cannot move too slowly.

Students take their cue from the instructor and they will learn much faster if they start with an optimistic attitude.

You may be afraid the students will be bored or insulted if you teach too slowly. Don't worry. *You cannot move too slowly.* Navigating through the system, in particular, is the most important part of your training. If the students leave your class with a thorough understanding of menus, icons, locating data, running reports, and how to get Help, they will be able to find their way though anything they need to do in the system.

If you rush through the dull material to get to the topics you find more interesting, you will appear to be nervous or uncertain of your material. If you rush because you are nervous or uncertain of your material, you may appear to be hostile toward your students, which will inhibit questions and create a negative environment. In other words, *you cannot move too slowly.*

Instead, take a lot of time to make sure that each student has a clear understanding of the basics. If you are uncertain of your knowledge in a particular area, openly confess your discomfort to the class. They'll respond with mild sympathy and you will have successfully placed yourself on their side, creating a "We're all in this together" atmosphere.

On-Screen Teaching

Follow your documentation as much as possible and indicate clearly when you move from one page to the next. Some people learn best by hearing, some by seeing and some by reading. You have to consider all learning styles to be an effective instructor.

When demonstrating tasks on the screen, and especially when leading the class through hands-on exercises, be sure to...

1. Move the mouse slowly and pause before clicking. The students don't know where you are going, so they may lose sight of the cursor on the screen. Think about how difficult it is to follow the puck when watching hockey.

2. Always use the mouse instead of a keyboard shortcut. It gives a visual indication of what you are choosing. For example, when selecting a menu option, move the mouse to highlight the selection, pause, then click to select.

3. Maintain a running commentary. Describe every step you take and every keystroke you enter. Your students are usually trying to follow you on their own terminals, so they are not watching your demonstration carefully. They are dependent

on your voice because their visual focus is divided between their terminals and your screen.

4. If you want to rush ahead on a step to make sure you are clicking the right button or option before you tell them what to do, go ahead. We all do it occasionally. But, be sure to go back and lead them slowly through the step. (Remember, nervous haste creates hostility and candid confession creates sympathy.)

Ask lots of questions and pay attention to the side conversations among the students, particularly during breaks. This will help you confirm that they understand the lessons covered and that the pace and clarity are appropriate.

Wake Up!

Watch your audience for yawns and drowsy nods. You are standing and talking, so you are likely to stay awake and focused much longer than the students. Announce a ten minute break at the first sign of restlessness or grogginess, especially after lunch. Don't worry that you are wasting valuable class time…they aren't learning when they're snoozing.

Even better than a break, but not always appropriate for every instructor or class, is to ask them to stand up, stretch, jump up and down, walk around in the room – basically to do whatever it takes to get the blood pumping to their brains again – and then sit down immediately and continue. We even had one class sing a song, which is a great way to get oxygen and blood moving, but this was a very special class.

Beware of the 40-minute lull. If the entire class drinks a cup of coffee together at 10am, the entire class will be alert for approximately 40 minutes, and then fall into a post-caffeine slump. Either encourage them to get another cup of coffee after 39 minutes, demand more participation from them to keep them alert, or be prepared to repeat most of the lesson later in the day.

After every break, start with a quick review. Get their attention focused by firing easy questions at them. For example, even on the third day of training, we will often ask, "What do you click to get the Help screens?", or "What do you click to Save your work?"

Answering simple questions builds confidence, gets everyone's attention back on you, and reinforces the most important information.

Put It In Context

As much as possible without unnecessarily stretching the class, teach each system task or activity in the context of a business process. Explain when the task will be performed during the students' daily routine and, if possible, who will be responsible for it.

What If Something Goes Wrong?

Training is usually the final test of your system before it is delivered into production. Therefore, you may encounter a bug in the application functionality that was not caught during project testing, or you may find that the class notices a problem with either data or screen options. In either case:

1. Don't panic. Make it very clear to the class that this is not an unexpected situation.

2. Explain if the instance you are using for training is not the same instance that will be used for production, so the data may be incomplete.

3. Emphasize the quality of testing that has been done by the Implementation Team, if necessary.

4. Take the opportunity to teach error-response steps to the class. Explain that, even in production, a few bugs may slip through and they should be prepared to document and report them.

5. Thoroughly document the system error and report it as soon as possible to the appropriate members of the Project Team.

If someone asks a question for which you have no answer, write it down and tell them that you will find out after class and get back to them. If it's a "What happens if...?" question, say, "I don't know. Let's try it." This is particularly useful if they are attempting to apply something they have learned on a different screen.

If it works, everybody learns something and you have successfully encouraged participation. If it doesn't work, you get the opportunity to teach error-recovery tactics before you add it to the list.

During breaks, find the right person on the Project Team to get the answers to your questions and to report errors, bugs and issues that have arisen during class. Be sure to follow-up on each question, even if you have to say, "Because I said so," or "Congratulations. You have stumped the teacher." One teacher we know kept a "Stump the Teacher" candy jar at the front of the room and threw a piece of candy to anyone who did. Use this carefully, as more obnoxious folks will just try to drain your candy jar instead of learning.

Manage the Attitude, Too

When you are trying to describe a benefit or improvement the new system will provide, it is best to demonstrate the functionality. This is not always possible, but it can be a very effective tool when available. Students often feel a certain amount of anxiety or resentment toward a new system, particularly when it affects a significant part of their job responsibilities. Any advantage you can show will alleviate part of this reaction.

Be aware that, for many students, learning a complex application is much more frightening than learning Outlook or Excel. In some cases, this is their whole job. If they can't learn it, they will be in trouble.

In every class, there are a few students who are secretly afraid that they can't learn to use the new system. You may know that anyone who can balance a checkbook or drive a car can learn your system, but don't tell them so. They'll think, "Yeah, right. Everyone but me," and be even more intimidated.

It's actually better to imply that learning will take time or be somewhat challenging. It will be easy for some, and they will feel pleasantly superior for being able to learn more quickly than others. Those who pick it up slowly will be reassured to know that others have had trouble, too.

Let *them* tell *you* that it's easy.

Training Evaluations

And, finally, don't let the class evaluations at the end of the session intimidate you. Remember that you are the only critic you really have to satisfy. We have gone into training sessions with excellent materials, thorough preparation and delivered a really great session...and then received bad reviews. We have also gone in without a clue, delivered a confused and rambling series of disconnected lessons...and received excellent reviews.

Through all this, we have learned that all we have to do is the best we can: prepare thoroughly, rehearse adequately, and deliver enthusiastically. Then, any positive or negative comments become useful guidance for the future and do not shatter our self-esteem.

Integrity Moves

In any career, trust is the basis for lasting relationships and trust is built on integrity.

A lot of people move into consulting because they have established a reputation in their industry as an expert, have a network of people who have called on them for help, and they would like to start getting paid for all the assistance they have been providing for free. This is a good reason to become a consultant.

Others move into consulting because they've heard that consultants make a lot of money. This is also a good reason to become a consultant, but you may not last long if that is the only reason you are doing it. There are many temptations facing consultants. Producing substandard work and fudging timesheets are only part of the picture.

The Integrity Moves are:

- Understand the *ethics* of consulting.

- Be willing to say, "*I don't know, but I'll find out.*"

- Be willing to say, "*I was wrong,*" when you find out you were.

- Be willing to say "*I did it,*" when you screw up.

- Give bad news quickly. Learn how to be a *Bulletproof Messenger*.

- Recognize that everyone eventually has *personal disasters on company time*. Manage your response to them so that the customer is not affected.

- *Manage expectations* in the people around you so that there are no surprises.

Protect your reputation for honesty and the money will follow. Get caught once in a shady transaction or violating the ethical ground rules and you'll soon find out how small the consulting world really is.

Ethics

The concept of ethics is difficult to define. Not necessarily in a dictionary sense, but in a way that communicates how to make decisions in our daily lives based on ethical standards. Most likely, your parents taught you the differences between right and wrong, mine and not mine, and generally how to be a good citizen. Unfortunately, a few years in business can make it seem like there is a gray area where you can do anything you want.

We decided to address this challenge by citing various examples relevant to the topic at hand. We will cite some common ethical dilemmas that are often encountered in the professional lives of consultants, and we will do our best to provide guidance on how deal with them. In addition, however, we will attempt to clarify some of the gray areas that are, while seemingly complex, actually fairly cut-and-dried in an ethical sense.

Non-Disclosure Agreements and Proprietary Information

As a consultant, you will see many documents and processes that are confidential and should never be discussed or distributed outside the company. In addition, you may see confidential internal information, like salaries or proposed organizational changes, that should not be discussed within the company.

Always be overly conservative with this type of material. You bear the responsibility for protecting your clients' interests and information more carefully than if it were your own.

The dilemma with non-disclosure agreements arises with things that don't seem to be company secrets. If, for example, you complete a cost accounting project at a potato chip factory in Dallas and then move on to a similar project at a greeting card company in Kansas City, you don't have to worry that the greeting card makers are going to ask for inside information on the potato supply chain. But they have engaged your services because you have experience with cost accounting processes and procedures inside manufacturing organizations, and they have seen your resume, so they are quite likely to ask you how the potato chip company accounts for items damaged in transit.

Whenever possible, particularly with topics like accounting procedures, keep your answers as generic as possible and refer to industry best practices or GAAP rules instead of the practices of one client or another.

Even if the information you are sharing is publicly available and complimentary, it's better to avoid identifying the client specifically by name. For instance, we might say that the friendliest and most passionately committed users we have ever trained were at a major bank headquarters in North Carolina, which couldn't possibly offend anyone.

If someone wanted to track down which bank we were talking about, they could probably figure it out by scanning our resumes, but why would they bother? The information they needed was included in the statement. If you develop this habit in all situations, regardless of whether there is an ethics question or not, you don't have to worry about accidentally violating an ethics rule later.

Non-Compete Agreements

It's a relatively common practice among consulting firms to bring in subcontractors on their project teams from other consulting firms. If you are an employee of Consulting Firm A and are "sublet" to Consulting Firm B for a particular project, a non-compete clause will undoubtedly be included in the subcontract agreement.

This means you cannot solicit work directly from the client, excluding Consulting Firm B from their legitimate share in the hourly rate. Customers may not be aware of these agreements, but it is your responsibility to avoid any impropriety by quickly squashing any discussion along these lines.

If circumstances arise that you believe make it acceptable for you to initiate a contract directly with the customer, your first call should be to your employer. Your company will need to secure a written release from Consulting Firm B, your contractual customer, before any further negotiations can take place.

The dilemma with non-compete agreements arises when you change projects within a client company or when you change employers. There is a temptation to think that the original firm that brought you into the client did not sell you to the new project team, you sold yourself, so it might be okay to exclude them from that deal. It's not.

If you change employers and then the client company contacts you directly and wants you back for more work, you might be tempted again to exclude the firm that originally sent you to that client. Still wrong. Call both your employer and your previous employer and let them know that you received the call. It's up to them to work out how the billing margin will be divided.

As former owners and managers of consulting organizations, we can tell you that these calls are appreciated and your reputation for integrity is enhanced.

Leave it up to the managers in question to decide whether they would rather do the paperwork to create a new subcontract relationship or to initiate a new client contract. Your goal should be to make sure that everyone knows what is happening and that your client's interests are served.

Drug Tests, Background Checks, Safety Training

Prior to starting a new assignment, you may be required to pass a drug test and/or background check and complete safety training provided by your customer. This is common in consulting and is not a reflection on you or even, in most cases, an indicator of the sort of work you will be doing. Even if you are going to work exclusively in cubicles and conference rooms, most manufacturing companies, for instance, require you to pass a test after completing warehouse and factory safety training.

Failing a drug test or background check, on the other hand, is a reflection on you. We aren't here to judge you on the decision to take illegal drugs, but you have an ethical responsibility to your employer to avoid embarrassing yourself or them. If there is any doubt that you will pass the drug test, don't take it.

Productization and Work-for-Hire

When a customer hires you to build a technology solution or produce a written document, they typically own the rights to that product exclusively.

Many consultants recycle parts of their work, chunks of code or bits of a training manual, from previous clients, but this is a tricky ethical area and if you have any doubts at all about your right to do so, check with your employer.

The general rule of thumb is that you can reuse sections from a document if you could recreate the material entirely yourself, given enough time. As with every other ethical question, it's better to be careful than to risk embarrassment, or worse.

In our experience, clients are happy to allow you to recycle generic products created on their projects, and they absolutely refuse to allow you to reuse anything that is, to them, a competitive advantage in their market. In other words, common sense is likely to prevail in this situation.

One other situation where you may be asked to use documents from previous clients is in proposal packages. The most common practice is to "scrub" the document so that it shows the type of information that would be included, but it is not possible to identify which client it was created for. This is a dangerous practice, however, and a lot of consulting companies have taken the time to create purely generic examples of their most common documents for use in proposals.

Recruiting

When you work side by side on a project team with employees in your client company, those employees will sometimes approach you about becoming a consultant. They've seen what you do and they've heard your tales from previous clients, and they want to be a part of the glamorous world of consulting. Can you blame them?

For you, this is an ethical problem because your client has invested time and money in training these people in the very same skills that make them appealing as consultants. Never actively recruit from your client site, and if someone approaches you, tell them that you are ethically barred from discussing employment with them. Don't worry. They won't be mad. They'll respect you for it.

If they quit their jobs and then contact you after you've left that particular client and moved on to another project somewhere else, refer them to your manager or HR Department. Give them the appropriate contact information and tell them to mention your name, if you like, but don't handle the recruiting activity yourself. Even after you leave the client site, there is an ethical gray area about these types of activities and it's safer to avoid it, if possible.

"Spin" vs. Truth

Possibly the most common ethical dilemma, while it is not often recognized as such, is using "spin" versus truth in communicating with clients. "Spin" is commonly used to mean either intentionally obfuscating or distorting the truth or deliberately avoiding a straight answer to a direct question. We've all heard politicians and actors (what's the difference again?) try to put a positive spin on the latest poor economic data or scandalous divorce. Consultants are often accused of not delivering hard messages to their clients in favor of maintaining good relationships.

The real goal of what we are calling "spin" is to communicate to your clients in a way that is palatable to them. Like adding salt to a bland dish or washing down bad- tasting food with good-tasting wine, "spin" should be thought of as communicating tough messages with good taste. With kindness.

Those who are sensitive to their client's appetite for bad news or tough messages will be more successful. Those who will, with purpose and foresight, frame the messages in a way that 1) allows the client to truly hear and comprehend the message and 2) gets the real message across, will be the most successful. You see, there is no ethical dilemma here.

It's not unethical to tailor a message to fit your client's personality; actually, it's unkind not to.

Deals - Over or Under the Table

You will encounter clients, both high-ranking and rank-and-file, who wish to make under the table deals with you. We have encountered this more times than we'd like to remember. Sometimes the quiet deal will involve asking for gifts, even small ones, where you know the gifts are an unspoken requirement for good relations. Some will even ask for kickbacks, and often boldly.

"If we hire you to do this job, I want 10% of the gross." "Bring in as big of a team as you want, but I'm taking 50% of the margin." "I'd like to hire you, but your competitor is going to buy my Porsche when this project is over." We did not make up any of these examples.

The ethical answer to such requests or demands is, hopefully, obvious.

Do not do under-the-table deals that benefit you or your client that you would not want exposed to scrutiny by executives of either party, lawyers, or courts. One former acquaintance of ours padded his pockets for years with backroom deals. He bought a big house, saved for his kids' college, bought a top-end motorcycle, a $150,000 sports car, and lived a lavish lifestyle. He also lost it all, including his family, when he was sentenced to eight years in prison for his criminal acts.

Do not get involved in these schemes.

In the ongoing spirit of direct communication with our readers, we'd like to add this: if reading about these backroom deals makes you want to get into consulting, put this book down and find another profession. We don't want you in ours.

Scenario: A consulting executive is hired as a virtual CIO (Chief Information Officer) responsible for driving a major technology project for a multi-billion dollar, global company. He is expected to build both an internal and a consulting team to drive the transformation that will result from the project. He hires every consultant through his company, and he keeps a piece of the hourly rate from every consultant hired. From the position of consultant/CIO, this person has direct hiring authority over the team and a huge ability to line his pockets, and he does. Is this ethical behavior?

This scenario is real, and surprisingly, the answer to the ethical question is yes. From the beginning, the CIO worked with the Board of Directors of the company to define the project and his role. He explained that he would be building the consulting team using his own company, and that he would benefit from doing so. Because he brought the deal above the table, the client and the consultant/CIO put controls in place to make sure the client was not taken advantage of, and they had a great working relationship throughout the project. The client had a successful project, and the consultant/CIO made a bunch of money legitimately. Everyone benefitted.

Scope Control and Change Orders

A huge area of ethical concern is often found in the area of scope control and change orders. The seemingly gray ethical area begins during the proposal process. Many consultants will define a very tight, limited scope in order to issue the lowest bid for a project, knowing that they will have to issue change orders along the way to successfully complete the project. Other consultants will whine and complain about this practice and feel that they were beaten by an unethical opponent when the other consultant wins the work.

Our advice to you is fourfold:

First, stop whining. Tough competition is part of being a consultant, and it is only going to get tougher. You are competing with a larger population of consultants than ever before with increasing levels of experience; you are competing outside your market area; you are competing globally.

Second, ask your potential client how they choose consultants. Often they will tell you that the lowest bid that appears to meet the objectives of the project is going to win. Sometimes they will choose based on the quality of the team, the detail of the proposal, or references from other clients. Some clients will not tell you anything about how they choose; we try to stay away from them. That's often code for "My cousin is bidding on the project; you don't have a prayer" or "I used to work for Big Consulting, Inc., and I trust them, so I'm getting these other bids to satisfy our procurement department."

Third, when compiling a bid without any guidance from the client, play fair, but play tough. There is nothing unethical about making a competitive bid. If you're willing to do the work to scope down your proposal and win the work, and then do the work later to get change orders approved, it's fair game. In your proposal, make your assumptions and scope clear so neither you nor the client have to argue over it later, but if they accept a tightly-scoped bid, that is their prerogative. To put it another way, Buyer Beware.

Last, and most importantly, do everything possible to build a working relationship with the client or potential client before selling anything to them. A level of trust will go a long way in helping you put together a winning proposal.

Scopes change, change orders happen, and responding to RFPs is very difficult work. Be truthful in your responses, and play the game hard. There is nothing unethical about that.

I Don't Know, But I'll Find Out

There are some rules for learning on the job. Different clients have different levels of tolerance for this, but you are always safe admitting you don't know something specific. No one can know everything.

On IT project teams, the consultant's role is often to be a technical expert and advisor. This creates an expectation in the customer's mind that you know everything and they'll ask the most outlandish questions with every confidence that you will know the answer.

Don't fall into the "I have to know everything to be a good consultant" trap. You cannot possibly know everything about any subject, even the one(s) in which you are supposed to be an expert. Real expertise comes from knowing how to find the answers.

> *Don't fall into the "I have to know everything to be a good consultant" trap.*

Learn how to say "I don't know, but I'll find out," with confidence. Believe it or not, your client will end up respecting you more for admitting you don't know, but only if you do find out the answer on a timely basis. As an added bonus, they'll often feel smarter for having thought of a question that stumped the expert.

If you have to ask your manager or a more experienced consultant for help finding the answer, also ask where they found it. Take this opportunity to learn something you don't know about resources that are available to you.

I Was Wrong

Authors' Note: We struggled with the title of this chapter. "I was wrong" has such a strong negative connotation. It could have been "I changed my mind" or "Now that I have more information, my opinion is reversed."   Other strong contenders were "Don't be afraid to flip-flop," and "Be willing to waffle," but we were reluctant to sound too political.

Too often, consultants fall into the trap of thinking they are supposed to know everything and never make mistakes. This creates a pressure on some consultants to be absolutely sure before they voice any opinion at all, and most project timelines don't have that much padding. Others respond by picking an opinion at random and then clinging to it like a life-raft long after the evidence against has started to pile up.

Express your opinion as your best guess based on the available information. If new evidence appears that suggests you were wrong, say so quickly.

Express your opinion as your best guess based on the available information. If new evidence appears that suggests you were wrong, say so quickly. It's more important that the right decision be made than that you look infallible.

On one project at Biggish, we were assisting the CFO with the design of a new chart of accounts. On one aspect of the design, we strongly urged that the decision be made one way and the CFO continued to resist. After a debate that lasted way too long, the following conversation took place.

Us: If we do it your way, it will create too many accounts.

CFO: I don't care how many accounts I have as long as I get the data I need! Why can't you understand what I'm saying??!?

We held out too long in this discussion and lost credibility with the customer before finally admitting that we were wrong and allowing the meeting to move to the next issue.

We've worked with many consultants who stubbornly refused to back down from an opinion no matter what. Sometimes the client stops listening and goes ahead with the logical solution. Other times, the client follows the consultant's (wrong) advice and later realizes that there was a better solution available. Every time, the consultant's credibility takes a hit and the client is poorly served.

Practice saying "I was wrong," with your co-workers, friends and family, until it comes easily. For some of us, this is a lifelong exercise, but it pays off in relationships much better than being right. Remember, no one likes the smartest kid in the class. Okay, that's probably not true. (Calm down.) On the other hand, it definitely IS true that customers trust a consultant who is willing to admit when he is wrong.

I Did It

A highly frustrating situation a project manager faces is when a problem mysteriously appears in code that worked perfectly yesterday and everyone claims they did nothing to change it. He knows someone did it. He knows it can easily be un-done, if only he knew where a change had been made. If he's smart, he won't punish or embarrass the one who admits it. And yet, people still pretend they didn't.

Be the one who admits his mistakes. When one guy is hiding them, be the other guy. When you did something, even if you feel sure that it couldn't possibly have caused the problem that occurs, say so. Let someone else prove your action didn't cause the problem.

We did an upgrade project at Biggish, where one of the new features being introduced was an automatic, system-generated email notification that would be sent out to every hourly employee who had not submitted a timesheet by the weekly deadline. This is fairly simple technology and the application had a simple screen where the System Administrator could enter the text of the email notification and details about when it should be sent.

> *Be the one who admits his mistakes.*

We tested the functionality in advance and even did a Biggish-wide publicity campaign about the notifications, including the information that the email would be sent at midnight on the day that timesheets were due, every Friday, and that emails would continue to be sent to each delinquent employee until their timesheets were submitted.

You already know what happened, don't you?

The admin screen contained choices for the interval between reminders. The choices were something like minute, hour, day and week. The System Administrator who set up the notification in Production went too fast and accidentally clicked to select "Minute".

At midnight on the first Friday after we went live in Production with the upgraded system, it automatically generated several hundred email notifications for the employees who had not submitted timesheets. At 12:01, another notification was sent. And again at 12:02. By Saturday afternoon, and it's a testament to the Biggish network administrators that it took so long, the network was jammed and email was completely shut down.

The project team was summoned from their various weekend activities and the shouting began. The CIO at Biggish was a former Marine who knew how to yell. His whole head would turn red and he would lean down until his face was inches away from yours and he would shout until the veins in his neck throbbed. That day, he was shouting at the Project Manager, who honestly had no idea what could have caused the problem. Everyone else in the room was understandably silent. Until...the bravest System Administrator we have ever met stood up and said, "I did it."

He didn't try to explain his mistake until the shouting, now directed at him, was over. He simply stood there and took it. When he finally did get a chance to explain, he did not offer any excuse. He started with a sincere, heartfelt apology, and then explained what had happened and how he had corrected the mistake. He then offered to stay and help the network administrators clean up the mess.

The CIO never forgot that System Administrator's name. He was promoted early and often, and is now a CIO himself, though at a Smallish company, where he hardly ever yells at his project teams.

On another project, we were hired to build a custom financial reporting system at Biggish, and after their first year-end close, the Biggish CFO called us up and told us that our financial reports were clearly wrong because they did not match what he was sure his numbers were supposed to be. We scrambled to fix the reporting tool.

At the same time, Biggish was migrating balances from a legacy, mainframe system into the packaged financial system (which we had implemented along with the financial reporting system). We knew they were having challenges in mapping and moving the data, but that is normal, and Biggish's talented team was working diligently on it.

We dug deep into the financial reporting tool and determined that it was accurately reporting the numbers that had been properly entered into the financial system. When we took this message to the CFO, he slung the red-lined reports at us and screamed, "This is a [consulting company] problem!"

We struggled for several more weeks, and billed a whole bunch of hours, only to prove over and over again that our reporting system was giving the right answers based on the journal entries entered in the financial system.

Finally, after the CFO had also tried for weeks to resolve this issue within his team, he admitted to us privately that, on his instruction, the legacy migration team had manually entered balances directly into the general ledger (instead of properly entering journals), which caused the huge discrepancies between his reporting and ours.

Had he admitted taking this action sooner, we could have included a plan to accommodate the discrepancies in our reporting from the beginning. Instead, we spent weeks and hundreds of thousands of dollars trying to fix an unfixable problem.

Bulletproof Messenger

Too often on projects, individuals or groups hide the fact that there are problems. This prevents the Project Manager from being able to manage the problem and protect the relationship with the client. It also means you don't have the rest of the team or your chain of command to help you solve the problem.

Even though people often shoot the messenger, tell them anyway. Be a Bulletproof Messenger who doesn't mind getting shot if it means that everyone knows what they need to know.

There is one key strategy to being a Bulletproof Messenger. Always tell the truth. Every single time.

> *There is one key strategy to being a Bulletproof Messenger. Always tell the truth. Every single time.*

Furthermore, you have to be right and you have to say it to the right people.

You won't win any points for running around telling everyone that the sky is falling when they can plainly see that it isn't. On the other hand, if you cultivate a reputation for being the one who is willing to say that the emperor has no clothes, and if you whisper it in the emperor's ear instead of shouting it from the rooftops, he'll thank you instead of shooting you. Probably.

We all learned this lesson in Kindergarten and again several thousand times before we finished high school, but it bears repeating in this context.   In consulting, there are many temptations to stretch the truth, edit the facts and generally tell it the way we wish it was.

We did one project where our assignment was to implement three applications in a corporate-wide system that was used to manage

117

financial transactions across the entire company. The applications in question related to fixed assets, project accounting and accounts receivable (AR). The first step was to validate that the company would be able to manage its asset, project and AR transactions using the vendor's applications without extensive customization and we quickly discovered that it would not.

The client sold its products through wholesale and retail channels and the vendor's AR application was not, at that time (a long, long time ago), capable of performing both of those transactions. Retail or wholesale, but not both.

We were under a great deal of pressure from the software vendor, and from our internal leadership, to say it could be done, and we worked hard to find a solution. We talked to experts with more experience. We consulted system architects about integrating two separate instances, so that the separation was invisible to the users. In the end, the only way that particular vendor's product could be used would be if (a) the company completely changed the way it did business, or (b) we customized the application to the point that it would be cheaper to build a new one from scratch.

In the end, with the support of a battalion of experts, we had to break the news to the vendor and to the client that the project simply was not feasible. Because we had done our homework and demonstrated our commitment to a solution before presenting our findings, the anticipated uproar didn't happen. Everyone accepted the information as presented and immediately moved on to looking for another solution.

The relationships our firm had built with the vendor and with the client were protected and actually strengthened as a result, as our reputation for being willing to tell the unpopular truth made us more trustworthy in future negotiations.

One More Reason to Admit Problems

Studies have shown that customer satisfaction is not measurably improved by good performance. If your client has high expectations when you start an activity, your successful execution of the task will result in an evaluation that sounds something like, "We have no complaints. He was fine." It may surprise readers of Dilbert to learn that this is the feedback most consultants and consulting firms hear after most consulting engagements.

On the other hand, those same studies have determined that customer satisfaction skyrockets when a problem arises and is resolved.

You have seen this in action. If you go to a restaurant and your meal is served as you ordered it and in a reasonable time, you are satisfied. This is the result you expected when you selected the restaurant. If you go to a restaurant and your meal is incorrect or the service is slow, your satisfaction dips. At that point, the experience can go one of two ways. The waiter or manager can ignore your problem or rudely refuse to solve it, which will sink your satisfaction level significantly. Or, they can quickly serve the correct meal with a charming apology and win your enthusiastic loyalty.

Now imagine that the waiter in question realized your meal had been prepared incorrectly and resolved the problem before it ever reached your table. You are unaware of the issue and your satisfaction remains at its original level. You have no complaints. He was fine.

We are not suggesting that you create problems to solve, or that we would encourage waiters who brag about how efficient they have been, but this information definitely supports the premise that you must report issues as soon as you are aware of them.

If you hide them and try to resolve them yourself, the best possible outcome is that satisfaction stays the same. If you report and resolve them publicly, satisfaction will go up. Of course, this requires that you resolve the issue, but that's your job. You were going to do that anyway.

Personal Disasters on Company Time

Consulting is just like any other job, real life happens while you are at work. Accidents, illness, weather disasters and holidays can all create problems that are compounded if you are away from home and your personal support network.

If you work as a consultant on site with your clients most of the time, you may not feel the typical employer-employee connection with the staff at your consulting firm, but if a crisis arises, these are the people you should turn to for help first. As consulting managers, we've received calls from consultants who:

- Were stuck at the border with expired work visas, unable to get back into the United States

- Were traveling and had received word that their homes were flooded, on fire or being evacuated because of a hurricane

- Had been in car accidents and were injured

- Had been arrested for DUI, public intoxication or solicitation

In every case, we immediately responded with every assistance we could offer. We never said, "This is not our problem. Solve it yourself." Even so, it is much more common for a consultant to try to solve the problem himself, or worse, to involve the client, than to call his employer for help.

Christine's Hurricane Story

I was scheduled to teach a week-long class in Orlando, as a hurricane was headed straight for that part of Florida. When I boarded my flight to Orlando on Sunday afternoon, the news coverage and weather reports were still a bit vague about where the hurricane would come ashore, but common sense should have told me to stay home. If common sense spoke, I wasn't listening.

I arrived in Orlando, checked into my hotel and turned on the television, only to discover that Hugo was now expected to hit Orlando Tuesday afternoon. This was a big hurricane and the people in the city were boarding up their windows and packing their cars. Still, I pretended it wasn't happening.

On Monday morning, I hopped in my rental car and drove to the client site just as originally scheduled. Please note that I did not call my consulting manager, my client, or even my mother, for advice.

When I arrived at the site, the people there were busily packing up servers and nailing plywood to the windows and doing all the things you do in preparation for leaving town and watching the hurricane on television from a safe distance. They were astonished to see me and their words can be summed up as, "Are you out of your mind????"

I called my manager in Washington, D. C., and was told, "Get your things, check out of your hotel, drive directly to the airport and get on the first plane going anywhere. Call me when you land and we'll figure out how to get you home from there. Oh, and you're an idiot."

The Orlando airport was a madhouse. Several cruise ships had docked at the Port of Orlando and dumped all their passengers into the airport, also without tickets or reservations to go anywhere. I was lucky enough to get on a flight to Dallas within a few hours, but I will never forget standing in that crowd at the ticket desk and wondering if I was going to spend the next few days trapped in the Orlando airport. I felt silly for being in Florida at all and was painfully aware that I should have stayed home.

Christine's Blizzard Story

Only a few months later, while still working for the same consulting manager, I was working on a project in Denver with several other consultants, all of whom were much more familiar with winter weather. Our normal weekly routine was to fly into Denver on Sunday evening and fly out on Friday afternoon. We had been doing this for several months.

This particular week, the weather reporters on television started getting excited on Tuesday about the forecast. They used words like "record snowfall predicted" and "blizzard conditions", and warned people to begin preparing for a serious storm that would hit on Friday. Mindful of the Orlando hurricane incident, and particularly of the atmosphere in the airport that day, I called my manager and presented him with a choice. I would either go home early and miss two billable days of work, or I would go ahead and make plans to stay in Denver over the weekend, at the company's expense. We decided I would stay in Denver.

On Wednesday evening, I went to a discount store to buy warm, snuggly sweats and slippers, and then to a bookstore where I bought a stack of paperbacks to keep myself entertained all weekend. Finally, even though I was staying in a four-star hotel, I went to a grocery store and stocked up on snacks and Diet Coke. For some reason, I also bought a flashlight.

When the storm hit early Friday morning, the city was blanketed in snow. You may have seen it on the news. The Denver airport was closed, but full of people who couldn't go anywhere. The city was paralyzed for two days.

At the hotel, and this is one of my favorite road warrior stories, the staff was limited to a skeleton crew because the roads were closed, so guests were encouraged to fend for ourselves. A poker game went on in the bar for, as far as I know, the whole two days, with players coming and going as money ran out. The bar and restaurant were fully stocked, so the essential supplies held out, but we had to make our own beds (like that happened!) and pick up clean towels in the lobby. Meals were served buffet style and total strangers ate together and shared life stories. Many people appeared in pajamas, as not everyone thought to augment their professional wardrobe with sweatpants before the blizzard.

All in all, it was a great experience for me. Not so much for my colleagues. One guy went to a hockey game with some friends on Thursday night and ended up with his rental car in a snow bank near his friends' house and had to walk a couple of miles in the storm. Another guy spent the weekend sleeping on the floor at the airport.

Christine's Gunfire Story

On one client site, the consultants were assigned a conference room near the main entrance. One day, for reasons that would give away too much information about the client, a member of the general public came into the main entrance and began firing a handgun. From our conference room, the sound of the shots was deafening and we knew the shooter was nearby.

The entire team froze for a moment and then scrambled to hide. In the midst of shrieks and shouted instructions, there was the sound of laptops hitting the floor because power cords were caught on their owner's shoulders as they dove under the table.

One guy ran to the door to find out what was happening. As it turned out, the situation was resolved quickly and no one was injured, but the lesson here is: Be the one who hides, NOT the one who goes to find out what is happening!

A Note About Fire Drills and Bomb Threats

Every corporate client you visit will have a disaster response plan posted somewhere, usually near the elevators. Even if you only plan to be there for a few weeks, you still have to learn it and participate in whatever drills take place. We know this should go without saying, but there is always one consultant who thinks their work is more important than standing in the parking lot while someone does a headcount. It's not.

Why This Is An Integrity Topic

National and personal disasters will happen to everyone sooner or later. The way you handle them, as a consultant, is a matter of common sense and integrity. You are responsible for your own safety and for keeping yourself out of harm's way. You are also responsible for communication with your employer.

When Hurricane Katrina hit New Orleans, we were working for a consulting firm headquartered just outside the French Quarter. Many of our colleagues lived and worked in New Orleans and the company hosted client data on servers in the building. When it became clear how big and strong this storm was, staff members loaded servers and file boxes into their own cars and headed for Tennessee, Illinois and Texas.

Katrina was a horrible disaster that affected thousands of people, but we were struck by the commitment required from those staffers at our company who took the time to rescue hardware and take it with them as they evacuated the city. During the first two weeks after the storm, we had a company-wide daily conference call where the president conducted roll call, trying to locate missing employees, gave out information about various rescue efforts, communications and insurance claims, and presented his personal assurance that the company was primarily interested in the safety of its people.

Those who could continue billing did so. Those who lost their homes and couldn't work continued to be paid, and many were housed in the homes of company executives who had extra space and weren't affected by the storm. No one who was able to work took advantage of the opportunity for time off with pay. The clients who had their service interrupted were not billed for downtime. During the corporate financial crisis that followed losing our headquarters, not one single employee was laid-off and no one missed a paycheck.

Companies and people will rise to the occasion and show integrity in a crisis. If you find yourself in one, don't hesitate to ask for help, whether your crisis is a wrecked rental car or a broken arm or a flooded house.

Manage Expectations

We heard a story once about a boy who was in a terrible car accident where he lost his left arm. Once he recovered physically, his parents felt he needed something to give him physical and mental confidence living without his left arm. They signed him up to study judo under a wise master, called a sensei. The master taught him basic stances, but only one move.

He practiced and practiced, but always this one move. After a few months, he asked the sensei if he could begin to learn other moves so he could compete in tournaments. The sensei said, "No. You only need this one move." Wanting to be a good Grasshopper, the boy trusted the sensei and continued to practice the one move until he mastered it.

Eventually, the boy entered his first tournament, where he easily won his first two bouts. The third was harder, but he eventually pinned his opponent with this one move and won.

Victory followed victory, until the boy was in the final bout for the tournament championship, where he was matched against an opponent who was much bigger, stronger and more experienced in judo. After a few minutes, the referee stopped the bout and suggested to the sensei that he should pull the boy out of the match, saying "He could get hurt."

The sensei said, "No. Go on."

The boy finally won the bout and the tournament, pinning the bigger, stronger opponent with his one move.

On the way home in the car, the boy asked the master, "How could I win the whole tournament with only one move?"

"Your move is one of the hardest and most advanced moves in judo, and you have mastered it," the sensei replied. "There is only one known defense against this move, and it requires your opponent to grab your left arm."

If you only master one move in this book, make it this one. Successful consulting is two parts setting expectations properly and one part execution.

You already know the damaging effects of poor expectation management. When someone says, "I'll be there," and then doesn't show up, you may let it slide once or twice. After multiple no-shows, however, you stop trusting that person. When they say, "I'll be there," you automatically think, "No, you won't," even if you don't say it. Wouldn't you prefer that he say, "I want to be there and I'll try, but there are two other things that might interfere," so that your expectations are set properly?

If you only master one move in this book, make it this one. Successful consulting is two parts setting expectations properly and one part execution.

This is also true with consulting project expectations.

If you are asked to estimate how long it will take to create a particular report, for example, and you believe that it will take 16 hours to do it, don't quote "two days" with the assumption that you'll be able to focus all your attention on this work for the entire two days. Distractions like meetings and meals will interfere with your work, even if you are exactly right about how long it will take. In this case, estimating three days is reasonable.

If there are several variables that might delay completion beyond your three-day estimate, go further and say "three to five days, depending on..." and list those variables. This is not sandbagging, which is bad. This is clear communication, which is good.

If you are conservative with your estimates, you leave yourself room to finish within your timeframe even if some of the variables go against you. Sometimes, however, everything goes wrong. A conservative estimate doesn't anticipate every possible problem, so you'll have to revise your estimate partway through the work. This is where you realize the benefit of managing expectations.

If you originally said, "It will take three days to complete this report," with no caveats or conditions, you haven't left yourself any wiggle room. On Day Two, when you realize that you are going to need at least another three days to resolve all the problems you have encountered, you have to deliver bad news to the project manager. If, on the other hand, you have already identified a bunch of potential problems, then it's much easier to ask for more time. You aren't delivering bad news, you are simply providing a status update.

The resulting impact to the project schedule may be the same, but the tone of the conversation is totally different, and you won't walk away with the stink of failure all over you.

Project Timelines

One of the Project Manager's jobs is to manage the overall timeline of the project, which often means combining task estimates from lots of different people and mapping them to a single delivery date. Different Project Managers approach this task in different ways. Some will generously pad every estimate to guarantee the success of the project. Others will shave every estimate to provide an optimistic forecast at the beginning of the project.

Neither of these approaches is wrong, and sometimes one extreme or the other is required by conditions at the client site.

We did one project at Biggish where the Director in charge of the project said, "The consultants have overrun their dates and budget on the last six projects here. Right now, we have a zero-tolerance for overruns. Don't give me a date you can't make, no matter what happens." We padded that project plan to the point where we could have done three or four projects in the timeframe allotted, which was exactly what the client wanted.

As we completed phases of the project early, we continually revised the timeline with the client, so that when we finished two months early, no one was surprised. Throughout the project, we managed his expectations carefully so that our conservative estimates never sounded like lies.

On another project with the same client, a different Director told us, "I can't approve this project if the timeline extends beyond the end of Q4. The budget for next year isn't set yet and I can't commit to spend money that hasn't been allocated."

Our response was, "If everything goes exactly right, if no one gets sick or takes a vacation, if every manager shows up for every meeting, if every approval is granted quickly, and if all the requirements have been identified and stay exactly as they are now, we can finish before the end of the year."

He said, "Great. Give me a proposal that says all that. We'll do change orders to cover everything that goes wrong, after next year's budget is approved."

The team members on this project were not aware of this conversation and it would have been inappropriate for us to share it with them, but we did say that our timeline was a best-case scenario and that the client knew that.

Talking to the Client

President Lincoln said, "The world will little note, nor long remember, what we say here," in the Gettysburg Address, which is one of the most quoted speeches in American history. He wasn't being sarcastic. He really believed that his few remarks that day would be quickly forgotten.

In any project role, you will have some contact with the client. Even in seemingly innocent, off-the-record conversations, what you say will be noted and remembered.

- Never say "easy", unless you're talking about an Easy-Bake Oven. Nothing in consulting is easy; that's why the rates are so high.

- Watch everything you say.

- Watch everything you publish even more closely than what you say.

Clients will remember due dates, percents complete, and any other optimistic statements regardless of whether they are founded or not.

Over-Promise Means Under-Deliver

One day at Biggish, a user called one of the project consultants for help with a database query. In passing, the user said, "It sure would be easier if we had a report that would give us this information."

Anxious to help and mindful of the need for a good relationship with the user community, the consultant said, "We can do that! Heck, I could create that report this afternoon," which was perfectly true. However, it didn't take into account the project's scope control and change management process, the consultant's previously assigned tasks for the afternoon, or the question of whether the same report could be slightly changed to meet other users' needs as well.

When the consultant reported back to the Project Manager that he had promised a custom report to the user, all these issues were brought to his attention and he had to go back to the user and say, "I'm sorry, I should not have made a promise like that without checking with the project team," which created bad feelings between the user and the project team that did not completely evaporate when the report was created later that week.

If you are prone to exuberant promises, at least learn to put conditions on those promises immediately after you make them. If a bell had gone off in that consultant's head when he said, "We can do that! Heck, I could create that report his afternoon," he might have saved the situation by saying, "Oh. Wait. I'm always doing this, and it's not fair to you. I can't promise to do the report right away. There are probably a lot of other things to consider that I don't know about. But it's definitely possible to put this into a report, so I can promise to try."

This way, if the report could be created right away, the consultant looks like even more of a hero, and if not, the user's expectations have been set so that there are no hard feelings. Set the expectations so that you aren't a failure if nothing changes.

Even simple statements like, "Everything is on schedule," can be harmful if they aren't true. Either you don't know what is going on or you are lying. If they are true, no one will remember that you said it.

Administrative Moves

A lot of the consultants we have worked with are in consulting as a second career. After retiring from the corporate ladder with years of accumulated experience and expertise, they found that they weren't ready for days filled with golf and bridge, so they returned to work. As consultants, they have found greater freedom to choose where and how they will work.

The most difficult part of this transition is often the administrative work required from consultants. When you were a senior vice president at a global firm, you probably didn't have to fill out a timesheet every week or document every decision you made. As a consultant, you do.

The Administrative Moves are:

- Understand that *if it's not written down, it didn't happen*.

- Always *bill what you work and work what you bill*. And if you don't, understand the unwise risk you are taking and be prepared for the consequences.

- Issue complete and timely *status reports*.

- Document *action items* so that they result in action.

- Document *assumptions, risks and issues* so that everyone involved understands and there are no surprises.

We touched on this topic briefly with the rule that said Do the Easy Stuff Perfectly, but not all administrative work is easy. Nevertheless, it is important. Documenting your work immediately, completing status reports and timesheets accurately, writing action items and issues correctly...all these things should become a matter of routine or habit so that you don't have to think about it at all.

As Nike says, Just Do It.

If It's Not Written Down, It Didn't Happen

The written word is important in many professions, and there are a variety of axioms used to describe it.

Journalism: Word becomes Truth.

Law: If you didn't write it down, you didn't do it.

Politics: If you are not doing the writing, then you are at the mercy of who is.

Consulting: If it's not written down, it didn't happen.

We would like to expand the consulting axiom above about documentation to include: If they don't understand it, it's not written down right.

The harsh reality is that unless you can produce documentation to validate your contributions in a consulting engagement, you run the risk of being perceived as useless. The worst case scenario is that the client refuses to pay for your time or expenses because they cannot see that you accomplished anything.

Signature Approvals

One of the advantages your client gains when they bring in consultants is the ability to enforce structure and discipline on the internal staff as well. When you complete a Requirements document or Solution Design, you can demand that the interested parties sign it to provide proof of their support and participation.

Clients are notoriously reluctant to officially state that any phase of a project is complete and insisting on signature approvals may be the only way you can manage your progress and maintain your schedule.

Email Confirmation of Exceptions to Rules

If you are given verbal instructions to deviate from your contractual obligations or to proceed without the necessary signatures, it is common practice to insist on email confirmation of those instructions. This might be summarized as "If they aren't willing to write it down, they probably don't really mean it."

Escalating Issues and Reporting Problems

Throughout the Communication section, we talked about the importance of keeping your chain of command informed about problems and issues. Hallway conversations are not sufficient protection against hearing "Why didn't I know about this?" Send an email, include the issue in your status report, document it on the issue log, AND mention it during at least one hallway conversation.

The harsh reality is that unless you can produce documentation to validate your contributions in a consulting engagement, you run the risk of being perceived as useless.

This won't protect you against being blamed for causing or failing to solve the problem, but it will ensure that you don't carry the whole responsibility alone.

Re-Assignment of Tasks

If you are assigned ownership of a task in writing, you own it until it is re-assigned in writing. We've seen many consultants squirm in status meetings when asked about the status of a task that they thought was re-assigned to someone else.

"Tentative, Preliminary, Draft"

Along with "Proprietary and Confidential", "Not Intended for Distribution", and "Strawman", these words can save a consultant's project, client relationship, or even career. Use them liberally on introductory pages, footers, and watermarks throughout any and all documents, even when they're finalized, signed-off, justified, and agreed-to. Only take them off when specifically requested by the client. Then, if at all possible, get a signature, or at least an email from the client saying they support the decision to "finalize" it.

This will protect you and encourage the client to understand the decisions they are making before the end of the project.

Bill What You Work, Work What You Bill

Our paychecks depend on our timesheets and invoices, whether we are salaried employees or independent contract consultants.

Bill What You Work

If you are a salaried employee of a consulting firm, your company is required to pay you whether you complete your billable-hour timesheets or not. But if you don't complete your timesheet on time, your employer can't invoice your client on time and they don't pay on time. In the long run, this makes it harder for your employer to pay you. Filling out your timesheet may feel like a low-priority chore to you, but it matters.

If you are an independent contractor, you are more likely to complete your timesheets or invoices on time, because you know you won't get paid until you do, but even contractors occasionally let more urgent issues trump the important task of billing.

Your time is valuable and your client should expect to pay for every hour that you work.

We were managing one project at Biggish where the budget was tight. Every hour and dollar was closely scrutinized and the monthly Invoice Review meetings with the client were tense, difficult sessions. Toward the end of the project, when it became clear that we could easily complete the work without running over the budget, the client relaxed and we, disastrously, stopped micro-managing the timesheet and invoice process with our team.

Two consultants on the team were independent contractors. With all the excitement and drama of the final phase of the project, both of them neglected to submit their invoices for the last two months until the project was over. In a Perfect Storm of neglect, we also failed to notice that their hours weren't included in our reporting or invoicing.

Weeks after the project was over, after celebrating our success and receiving kudos from the client for our financial acumen and diligence, these two very large, very late invoices arrived. The client eventually paid them, but only after expressing their disappointment in no uncertain terms. Our firm paid the contractors, of course, but we all learned a valuable lesson. The end result was that a wildly successful project was transformed into an embarrassing failure because everyone stopped paying attention to the timesheets.

Work What You Bill

Consulting engagements typically start slow. You may be required to be on site at a client location for weeks before your assigned tasks even start.

Do not assume that this is a mistake on the part of the client or project manager. They intend for you to use this time wisely so that you are ready to be productive when your tasks starts. Learn everything about the project and company you can. Form relationships with the people you will need when the pressure starts to build.

Another common challenge for consultants is the gaps between tasks during the project. We've often found ourselves working on a project, but at a loss for what to do next. You may have ten activities assigned to you and still reach a point where every single one is waiting on someone else to complete their task.

Go back to the 27 Moves and start thinking about what you are going to need to do when your work starts up again. Can you do any of it in advance? What kind of preparation will help you be more efficient when it's your turn?

If you are billing hours to the client, find a way to work during those hours. You may have to be creative in how you define "work", but reading white papers and learning about the challenges and solutions faced by other projects at your client site, or similar projects at other companies, is work. This is part of your job.

Exceptions to the Rule

Your time is valuable and your client should expect to pay for every hour that you work. On the other hand, there will be jobs where for some reason you can only bill forty hours per week, even though you have to work many more to stay on schedule. This usually occurs when budgets are fixed, timelines are fixed and the only way to succeed is to work a few hours for free.

People around you will be complaining about this. Don't join in. This is one of the realities of consulting, it doesn't happen often, and you can (hopefully) take comfort in knowing that you aren't staying late for free because you have to clean up an error you made. If you did create the problem, you must not only avoid complaining, you have to pretend you are happy to do it.

Overbilling your client is called "timesheet falsification" and it is a very serious infraction, usually punishable by termination. It's stealing, plain and simple. Don't do it.

Except...sometimes that's exactly what they want you to do. This is one of the times when the conflict between your many customers puts you in a situation where you have to make a judgment call.

Here are three examples, along with the justification and protective action taken. Just be aware that you are taking a risk, even if you are simply following orders issued by your manager, project manager and the CFO of the company. You remember the end of A Few Good Men, right?

Example 1:

The client had signed a contract with a consulting firm where the contract rates were to be charged on a per-month basis. Regardless of how many hours we worked, the client would pay the same monthly rate as long as we were assigned to the engagement.

The consulting firm subcontracted to us with hourly rates, where we would be paid only for the actual hours reported on our timesheets.

The Director responsible for overseeing our work and approving our timesheets refused to sign any timesheet with less than forty hours per week, reasoning that if his company had to pay for the time, the people sitting in front of him that he worked with every day, should receive the benefit. We complied with his instructions only after receiving an email from him stating that he would only approve timesheets that showed forty hours for every week.

Example 2:

A couple of years later, a different client engaged us to provide on-site support for an ERP system that had been fully implemented. There was no project, no deliverables and no fixed job responsibilities. The work varied from week to week, sometimes requiring long hours and late nights. During other weeks, there was nothing to do and very little reason to be in the office.

The Manager we reported to asked us to help him predict and control his costs by billing only forty hours each week, with the understanding that this would cause us to overbill some weeks and underbill others. The intent was that the overall result would be fair compensation for hours worked.

We also complied with this instruction, but we kept our own records of actual time worked, complete with detailed notes of what tasks were performed for whom. After six months, we were able to demonstrate that the average of the actual hours worked was within 5% of the hours billed.

Example 3:

A consultant we know was working on a project where, surprising everyone, his project deliverables were completed ahead of schedule. Weeks ahead of schedule, in fact. His firm was not pleased at the prospect of losing revenue and he was instructed to withhold the deliverables until their scheduled due date, and to continue going to the office and pretending to work.

This presented an ethical problem for our friend because he felt his client was being unfairly treated. After several days of soul-searching, he decided to risk being fired and talked to the project manager about his situation. In his particular case, this was the right decision, because the project manager was able to identify other project tasks that were behind schedule and to allocate his time to tasks he was qualified to do, thus providing his firm with the required billable hours and providing value to the project. But this could easily have gone the other way, and our friend was fully aware that he may be quitting his job when he opened the conversation.

Status Reports

On the first day, find out when status reports are due, in what format, and how they should be submitted. Get them done on time and be sure to include as much detail as possible, especially at the beginning of an engagement when you are establishing your credibility.

Status reports or progress reports may be formal, written communications or informal updates in a weekly status meeting. As with anything you do routinely, it's easy to fall into bad habits. Schedule a weekly appointment on your calendar where you set aside time to write your status report or prepare for your status meeting in advance.

Good status reports fulfill five critical needs. They...

1.   Communicate progress and document activities, which provides justification for your invoice and paycheck.

2.   Document action items, which ensures that everyone understands what you are expecting from them.

3.   Provide formal notification of the escalation of issues, which may spur new action from obstructive colleagues.

4.   Allow you to share responsibility for outcomes with your chain-of-command. (Yes, this is a weasel tactic, but keeping secrets is much, much worse.)

5.   Demonstrate discipline and a willingness to comply with project rules and requirements.

Status reports provide the customer who is responsible for overseeing your work with a sense of control. In the absence of detailed status reports, they often feel a need to micro-manage your activities. The worst-case scenario is when a customer asks,

"What have you been doing for the last few weeks?" and there isn't a ready answer already sitting in his Inbox.

We worked on one project where the team was large, the objectives were not clearly defined, and a great deal of time was spent in exploratory meetings where ideas were batted around but no decisions were made. In that case, we attached a copy of our weekly appointments printed out of the corporate email system to each status report. After only a few weeks, management recognized the cost of such meetings and bravely committed to project objectives and leadership decisions.

Action Items

Action items may be tracked in status reports, meeting notes or in a separate spreadsheet or database. Action items are the to-do list for the project team members, and writing an effective action item is a skill every consultant must develop.

An Action Item that will result in action contains the following elements:

- Description

- Assigned To

- Due Date

- Sufficient detail to allow the owner to understand the action

If you assign an Action Item to another member of your team, make sure they accept the assignment and commit to perform the action before the deadline *and* ensure that they understand the consequences of failure to act.

Not Good: Request more cubicles

Good: <u>Sally</u> – request more cubicles

Better: Sally – request more cubicles; <u>due</u> Tuesday, 5pm

Best: Sally – request <u>three</u> more cubicles; due Tuesday, 5pm

For an Action Item to result in action, it must be small enough to be performed by one person. If you have an Action Item that requires more than one person, it is either a Task that belongs on your Project Plan or an Issue that belongs on your Issues List until it can be broken down into individual Action Items. Tasks and Issues also have owners, to provide accountability, but they do not qualify as Action Items.

We've managed projects where the team members tried to insist that more than one person be assigned to particular action items. In many cases, there were good reasons for adding additional names to the action, but we have always held firm that one person must own the item.

Consider adding another column to your spreadsheet or tracking system that lists other people who are involved in the action, but you should always have one person who is ultimately accountable for making sure everyone does their part and the action is completed on time.

Assumptions, Risks and Issues

Assumptions are things that probably will happen. Risks are things that probably won't happen. Issues are things that have already happened, or need to happen urgently.

Assumptions

Throughout every project, you will have to write Assumptions in a variety of documents. In your initial project proposal document, you'll want to include assumptions like:

- [Client] staff and management will be available for, and will participate in, meetings with our team, given reasonable schedule constraints and sufficient advance notice.

- [Client] will provide access to workspace, conference rooms, network and systems, printers and other related logistical access.

- System requirements generally match the requirements outlined in the Request for Proposal.

- The Development Team's annual weekend trip to the Bahamas will not result in any lost work time or schedule delays.

In design documents, you may include assumptions like:

- Data in the existing order management system will meet the validation criteria of our standard interface.

- Customer and Supplier records have been reviewed and are free of duplicates. All invalid records will have been removed before the data is loaded into the new system.

- The Development Team can read English (or whatever language the specification documents will be written in).

Write assumptions as positive statements in the present or future tense.

Assumptions serve several purposes. They clearly define your expectations for the customer, and they establish the conditions under which you can most easily be successful. Finally, they provide some protection for your project in the event of timeline or budget slippage that is beyond your control.

Risks

Project managers track Risks that have been identified by the team members and report on the status of those risks to the project stakeholders, Steering Committee and Sponsor. Identifying project risks early and making sure those risks are visible to all interested parties is important.

Some fictional examples of project risks are:

- The roof sometimes leaks in the data center and heavy rain is predicted for go-live weekend, so the data might get wet while it is being loaded into the new system.

- Key users have pooled their resources and purchased Super Ball lottery tickets and the drawing is three days before the project's go-live date. If they win, they may not show up for work during the following week.

- The entire Development Team went to the Bahamas for the weekend. That was two weeks ago and they have not returned. Project delivery dates may slip as a result of the lost work time.

Write project risk statements so that the established facts are presented first and the potential impact to the project is a potential outcome of the facts. Every project risk should have a documented Risk Mitigation plan in place for how the project team will respond if the Risk becomes an Issue.

Issues

Issues have already happened and require action or intervention to be resolved. One of the most important tasks the project manager owns is tracking issues.

- The Development Team has notified us that they do not intend to return from the Bahamas. Replacement developers must be hired immediately.

Issues require solutions. Once a solution is identified, the steps required to implement that solution become either tasks on the project plan or Action Items assigned to specific individuals.

Every member of the team is responsible for identifying and documenting issues, and the project manager must report on issues and their associated resolution to the Steering Committee on a regular basis.

Red Flags

When there is a small problem, you have to identify it, report it, track it AND solve it. Throughout the process, you want to manage the level of panic in those around you. A "red flag" problem is just a problem, not a crisis or a disaster. For those, you don't need special words. People are always willing to name them. The key to using the "red flag" term is to make sure that everyone understands that it's just a warning. Something to keep an eye on.

Get Into Your Consulting Stance

We'd like to thank you for reading our book, and we hope you enjoyed reading it as much as we enjoyed writing it. We want to leave you with a few notes on how the principles in this book can be effectively employed every day on real consulting engagements.

First, keep this book handy. We kept it thin and non-repetitive with several purposes in mind. We wanted the book to be readable. We wanted it to be entertaining. And we wanted it to serve as a field guide that can be used in daily situations. We consult this book as a reference when, for example, we schedule meetings, coach new consultants, and when we start new jobs.

Second, especially when starting a new assignment, re-read critical parts of the book. As stated above, we avoided repetition in our writing (see what I did there?), and we tried to make every point as few times as possible. That being said, we all know the best way to learn is through repetition, so read the parts that taught you new things more than once, and read them again when new situations arise.

Third, share these principles (and, hopefully, a copy of the book) with people you work with or are likely to work with regularly. Having a common language and a baseline understanding of the principles in this book will help you and your colleagues to lift each other up and help you to far exceed your client's expectations.

Last, try to be perfect, but do not expect to achieve perfection. You'll only frustrate yourself and those around you, and you'll end up being cynical. The true measure of a person is how well they respond to inevitable adversity. Every engagement has crazy people (because, you know, people are involved), and every company has problems. Oh yeah...that's why we exist as consultants. Never forget that the existence of imperfection is your reason for having a job, and trying to eradicate it is your job.

Consulting Stance is an organization dedicated to building consultants' skills from the ground up. Starting with Everyday Practices of Extraordinary Consultants, we take those who are new to consulting or consulting concepts and help build their base of knowledge. We teach by talking about our mistakes and ways to avoid them. We teach seminars and do professional coaching, too.

Join the discussion on our website at www.consultingstance.com to further expand your horizons, put more tools in your toolbox, gather a little wisdom and hear more exciting tales from the road.

Words Consultants Use

One of the ways consultants emphasize their smartness is with specialized vocabulary. Due to the nature of our work, technical language and terminology is often necessary, but buzzwords tend to make you sound pretentious. On the other hand, if you are working on a team full of buzzword-addicted consultants, you'll need to fit in. Getting along with people sometimes requires speaking their language.

We've provided explanations for some common consulting lingo here, but this list is not comprehensive and the explanations provided are not scientific. The meanings of words and phrases evolve in the hands of experts (aka practicing consultants).

Boil the Ocean. This scope is too big to do in one project. Break it up into more than one. We often hear "We're not trying to boil the ocean here. We just need to..." when the client is trying to keep costs down and avoid an overly ambitious project scope.

Drink the Kool-Aid. To enthusiastically perform a task or follow a leader without knowing how this may affect you, or to buy the "company line" without question.

In business, you may hear someone say "He drank the Kool-Aid," when they mean, "He has been thoroughly trained in the program and we have his unconditional support," or "He is on board with our strategy." In political commentary, it is used to imply that people who disagree with you have been brainwashed or are under the influence of drugs.

Going Native. This is what happens when a consultant stops acting like a consultant and starts thinking they are part of the client organization. If you aren't willing to go somewhere else, go ahead and apply for a permanent job. You aren't providing the same value you were in the beginning.

Greenfield Instance. Clean, new installation of an application without customizations, configuration or data.

Holistic. We have no idea. We think it means a big picture view or a solution that includes upstream and downstream impacts. Whatever it means, it's a great consulting word and we use it a lot.

Paradigm. The perspective or view you have of a situation. For example, "When ownership of our order fulfillment project moved from Operations to Sales, it caused a paradigm shift that resulted in a whole new project strategy and approach."

Running in parallel. processing normal operating data through two systems simultaneously to compare performance and output.

When a client is feeling particularly paranoid about a new system that his consultants have developed or implemented, even after exhaustive testing and training, we will sometimes recommend running the new system in parallel with the old for a short period.

For an accounting system, we usually recommend one full accounting month. For systems that run manufacturing processes, a week is usually considered sufficient to find big problems that were missed during testing.

To get the full benefit of running in parallel, the users must perform all tasks in both systems exactly as they would if there were only one system running. (Yes, this means twice as much work for the users.) Since a new system often includes changes to business processes and different data, this is often impossible.

Strawman. First draft of a solution or proposal intended to provoke discussion

Consultants know that when a group is gathered to brainstorm a solution or craft a new business process, they need something to disagree with. A strawman is put forth with the understanding that every aspect of it could, and likely should, be changed or expanded.

In software design, a strawman design may be followed by a tinman, ironman and stoneman as a particular aspect of the design is gradually improved through collaboration. (Except for strawman, we've never personally heard these terms. We found this part in Wikipedia.)

Whatis.com provides the following definition: "In general, a strawman is an object, document, person, or argument that temporarily stands in for and is intended to be "knocked down" by something more substantial."

The word may have originated with a common political practice in the 1880's and 1890's when political leaders in the U.S. and across Europe would put a fake "man of straw" on the platform before making a speech. If the gathered populace threw rotten eggs or spoiled fruit at the fake, the politician would skip that public appearance and move on to the next town. This practice allowed them to avoid embarrassment and possible injury, but did little to improve public opinion.

Another possible source of the word is military training, where soldiers have always practiced bayoneting or shooting at targets shaped like men and often dressed like the enemy. Neither possibility seems more likely that the other and, in either case, the strawman is there to get hammered (stabbed, shot, beaten, burned,...).

Talking to the Dog. Thinking it through by talking it through out loud. You'll often hear engineers and programmers say that they finally solved a problem by "talking to the dog".

Use Case, n. A particular circumstance or situation in which the solution would be used. Use Cases are usually created, for all the different ways the system will be used by the Business Analyst as part of the early Requirements Gathering phase of the project. When designing a system, the engineer will refer to all the Use Cases that have been documented to determine if his solution will be effective in each situation.

When writing test cases, the system analyst will refer to the use cases to ensure that each one is included in system testing. When creating training documentation, the technical writer will also go to the Use Cases so that the training materials contain all the information needed to perform the task in every situation.

White paper. An authoritative report or guide published to share technical or business information, particularly related to solving common problems. Writing white papers is a great way for consultants to get exposure in their industry and develop a reputation for expertise.

Wireframe. Simple pictures that show a proposed user interface (UI), often used by business analysts to communicate expectations to users and developers. The word wireframe may refer to the black line that usually surrounds the graphic, but it may also refer to the wire models used in engineering design for things like buildings and airplanes.

Find Assets

Asset Number

Asset Name

Asset Description

Vendor Number

Vendor Name

Find   Cancel

We could write a whole book on the Words Consultants Use, and we probably will someday. In the meantime, this should give you something to think about and help you sound like a consultant.

Recommended Reading

There are so many great books out there about business, management, consulting, IT and professional development that it was hard for us to choose. We've limited ourselves to one from each author, though in many cases (like Jim Collins, Patrick Lencioni and Marcus Buckingham) we honestly think you should read every single word they've ever written.

Must Read:

Now, Discover Your Strengths
Marcus Buckingham and Donald O. Clifton | 2001

How to Win Friends and Influence People
Dale Carnegie | 1998 (first published in 1937)

The 7 Habits of Highly Effective People
Stephen R. Covey | 2004 (first published in 1989)

People Skills:

Strictly Business: Body Language
Jan Latiolais Hargrave | 2007

Life's a Campaign: What Politics Has Taught Me About Friendship,
Rivalry, Reputation and Success
Chris Matthews | 2007

The Anatomy of Persuasion
Norbert Aubuchon | 2007

Getting To Yes: Negotiating Agreement Without Giving In
Roger Fisher | 1991

Consulting Skills:

Case in Point: Complete Case Interview Preparation
Marc P. Cosetino | 2007

The Speed of Trust:: The One Thing That Changes Everything
Stephen M. R. Covey | 2008

Silos, Politics and Turf Wars: A Leadership Fable About Destroying
the Barriers That Turn Colleagues Into Competitors
Patrick M. Lencioni | 2006

Business Knowledge:

The Long Tail: Why the Future of Business is Selling Less of More
Chris Anderson | 2006

Made to Stick: Why Some Ideas Survive and Others Die
Chip Heath and Dan Heath | 2007

Built to Last: Successful Habits of Visionary Companies
Jim Collins and Jerry I. Porras | 2004

Skills Development:

Getting Things Done: The Art of Stress-Free Productivity
David Allen | 2003

Presentation Zen: Simple Ideas on Presentation Design and
Delivery
Garr Reynolds | 2008

The Back of the Napkin: Solving Problems and Selling Ideas with
Pictures
Dan Roam | 2008

Accounting for Dummies
John A. Tracy, CPA | 2008

Career Management:

What Got You Here Won't Get You There: How Successful People
Become Even More Successful
Marshall Goldsmith | 2007

Know-How: The 8 Skills That Separate People Who Perform from
Those Who Don't
Ram Charan | 2007

Useful Knowledge:

The Tipping Point: How Little Things Can Make a Big Difference
Malcolm Gladwell | 2002

Freakonomics: A Rogue Economist Explores the Hidden Side of
Everything
Steven D. Levitt and Stephen J. Dubner | 2006

The Dilbert Principle
Scott Adams | 1997

Leadership:

Who Moved My Cheese?: An Amazing Way to Deal with Change in Your Work and in Your Life
Spencer Johnson and Kenneth Blanchard | 1998

Fish! A Remarkable Way to Boost Morale and Improve Results
Stephen C. Lundin, Harry Paul, John Christensen and
Ken Blanchard | 2003

On Becoming a Leader: The Leadership Classic
Warren Bennis | 1989

If you are a traveling consultant, or if you've ever tried to read while walking on a treadmill, we enthusiastically recommend the **Amazon Kindle**. This new electronic gizmo makes it possible to carry hundreds of books with you on the road, turn pages with one finger, insert bookmarks or highlights as you read and look up words like "holistic" while you are reading.

Bravo, Amazon!!

About the Authors

Christine Lambden graduated from the University of Texas at Austin and then spent ten years sampling various jobs and entrepreneurial pursuits before landing, almost entirely by accident, in consulting. After a few years with Oracle Consulting, she jumped into the pool of boutique consulting firms in the Oracle Applications consulting field.

After seven years on the road, which included seven different employers and involvement in more than twenty implementations, she came back to Austin to rest. Here, she discovered a talent for coaching and mentoring consultants that proved valuable as a consulting manager, agency owner and, finally, author and speaker.

Christine lives in Austin, but still travels a great deal, often to teach , but sometimes just for fun.

Casey Conner was born in Texas City, Texas, and is a Texan through-and-through. He was raised in the small Central Texas town of Georgetown. Casey graduated with both a Bachelor of Business Administration and a Master of Science degrees in Finance from Texas A&M University.

Initially, he embarked on a career in consulting with Arthur Andersen Business Consulting in Houston, TX. Several months beyond being promoted to manager on an accelerated timeline, Casey left for the supposedly greener pastures of the dot-com revolution happening in Austin, TX as an internal consultant for a fast-growing software company.

After kicking out a horde of difficult consultants, rolling out a new financial system to 14 countries in 8 months, surviving at least 9 rounds of layoffs, and learning innumerable valuable life lessons, Casey moved on to a 30+ year old company as Director of IT, then returned to the software company to tackle several challenging projects that had failed in the past. After successfully completing those, he did a stint with a 65-person consulting organization as the Vice President of Consulting.

Eventually, Casey found his way home to a job as an independent consultant, entrepreneur and writer.

Casey lives in Austin, Texas with his wife, Kim, and their two children, Kalli and Cody, of whom they are very proud.

Consulting Stance Resources

Visit **www.consultingstance.com** for more information and to book training or coaching sessions.

Consulting Stance offers on-site training for professional services organizations and project teams:

- **Basic Consulting Skills Workshop** – 1-day workshop

- **Ask & Listen Workshop** – 4-hour training and practice session that allows participants to develop their skills and receive productive feedback

- **The Politics of Consulting** – 4-hour training session that allows participants to delve deeper into the skills required to manage and maximize their customer approval rating

Consulting Stance also offers 1-hour training sessions at your location or as a web seminar to accommodate teams and organizations that are scattered across multiple locations:

- **Managing Expectations**

- **Pick Your Battles**

- **Get Full Value From Every First Day**

- **Knock'em Dead Presentations**

For consultants, project managers and consulting managers who want a more personal, direct coaching relationship, weekly 30-minute telephone sessions are available at a reasonable cost. Consulting Stance coaching sessions are booked in 6-week packages to ensure the coach's availability for the duration of the commitment.

Printed in the United States
206855BV00002B/1-180/P